D1015760

Praise for *Fighting for Life*

"Lila Rose is one of the most courageous warriors for truth and life in America today. Her voice is indispensable. And in this book, you'll learn why she fights— and how you can fight too."

—BEN SHAPIRO, AUTHOR, POLITICAL COMMENTATOR, AND MEDIA HOST

"This book is so powerful! *Fighting for Life* invites us to live out our calling, to take risks, have courage, persevere, and be led by conviction. It contains great practical steps for readers no matter what their cause may be. Lila has taken on the greatest battle of our generation and mobilized multitudes to fight for the protection of the most marginalized, those human beings still in their mothers' wombs. I am thankful for Lila's strength and valor."

—CHRISTINE CAINE, AUTHOR, ACTIVIST, AND FOUNDER OF PROPEL WOMEN

"In a culture that casually disregards the most vulnerable, author and activist Lila Rose unpacks her transformation from conviction to catalyzing force in the pro-life movement. An honest and compelling recount of her courageous journey for justice, *Fighting for Life* will inspire us all to hear and heed God's great callings for us and boldly pursue them relentlessly, no matter the obstacle."

—BENJAMIN WATSON, FORMER NFL TIGHT END AND AUTHOR

"In the struggle against the greatest evil of our times—the institutionalisation of murder on a global scale—*Fighting for Life* may well prove to be one of the most important books you will ever read. It is an account of personal growth and a gripping tale of heroism that is both candid and humble. It reveals that grace is more powerful than the diabolic malice that denies the humanity of children in the womb and, ultimately, the humanity of us all. Standing as a sign of contradiction to this catastrophic blindness, Lila Rose's story, and mission, bears comparison to that of Joan of Arc and of David facing Goliath. It is not only a dramatic narrative; it is radiant with wisdom—the wisdom that heals."

—MICHAEL D. O'BRIEN, AUTHOR OF *FR. ELIJAH* AND *ISLAND OF THE WORLD*

"Lila is the definition of a fighter. Despite tremendous opposition, she founded one of the nation's leading pro-life and human rights organizations when she was just fifteen years old. Lila has refused to stay silent on issues that are plaguing our nation and the impact she has made in the abortion industry is astounding. Lila's story is a challenge for us all to take a stand, speak truth, and persist in the fight for life."

—LISA BEVERE, *NEW YORK TIMES* BESTSELLING AUTHOR

"Personal, practical, powerful—here's the compelling story of Lila Rose and how she became a pivotal leader of the millennial pro-life movement. Let her encourage and equip you to make a difference in whatever arena God wants you to serve. You'll be inspired by her passion, humbled by her honesty, and emboldened by her commitment to rescue the vulnerable. She can guide you to become, as she says, a force for change in a wounded world."

—LEE STROBEL, *NEW YORK TIMES* BESTSELLING AUTHOR

"Lila Rose is one of the most fearless, powerful women I've ever met. I'm so grateful that she's shared her story in these pages, as I have no doubt it will inspire countless young women to be courageous enough to make a change in the world."

—JEN FULWILER, STANDUP COMIC AND BESTSELLING
AUTHOR OF *SOMETHING OTHER THAN GOD*

"An inspiring account, and a must-read not just for those in the pro-life movement, but all those who believe they have been created to make a difference!"

—CURTIS A. MARTIN, FOUNDER OF FOCUS

"This is the true book of 'rules for radicals.' Lila Rose shows us that the most authentic revolutionaries are those who are most completely converted. Her book is challenging, but I need the challenge. Maybe we all do."

—SCOTT HAHN, AUTHOR AND THEOLOGIAN

"This is a book that should be put into the hands of every young person who is looking for a cause worthy of a total, lifelong, passionate commitment. Its story line is compelling, and its lessons—its practical and 'personalist' principles—are tested, tried, and true, but forgotten and flaunted by a society suffering from both amnesia and anemia, i.e. lacking both identity and blood (life and passion)."

—PETER KREEFT, AUTHOR AND PROFESSOR OF PHILOSOPHY
AT BOSTON COLLEGE AND THE KING'S COLLEGE

"When future generations look back at our time and wonder how we could have allowed so many unborn children to die and so many women to be exploited by abortion, they will look to heroes like Lila Rose and know that we were without excuse. *Fighting for Life* will inspire and motivate you to be one of those heroes— and to bring that future closer today."

—KAREN SWALLOW PRIOR, AUTHOR OF *ON READING WELL:
FINDING THE GOOD LIFE THROUGH GREAT BOOKS* AND *FIERCE
CONVICTIONS: THE EXTRAORDINARY LIFE OF HANNAH MORE*

"Lila Rose's engaging and vividly written memoir offers far more than a leading pro-lifer's personal story: It's full of practical lessons for all men and women of conscience who seek to change our troubled world for the better."

–SOHRAB AHMARI, AUTHOR OF *FROM FIRE, BY WATER: MY JOURNEY TO THE CATHOLIC FAITH* AND *THE UNBROKEN THREAD: DISCOVERING THE WISDOM OF TRADITION IN AN AGE OF CHAOS*

"For fifteen years Lila Rose has brought visionary leadership and courage to the pro-life convictions of millions of Americans. In this book, with her unique and relatable blend of advice, anecdotes, and spiritual reflections, Lila shares sound direction for anyone wanting to change the world and themselves—and she introduces the reader to the wise, kind, and brave heart of a woman whom many of us have been privileged to know and love all along."

–DAVID DALEIDEN, FOUNDER OF THE CENTER FOR MEDICAL PROGRESS

"The pluck, determination, and passion for defending life that have made Lila Rose a force to be reckoned with are evident on every page of this spirited, engaging guidebook. Bravely sharing her struggles as well as her successes, her weakness as well as her strength, Lila offers us a powerful reminder that who we are matters even more than what we do and the greatest force for social change is a heart transformed by grace."

–COLLEEN CARROLL CAMPBELL, AWARD-WINNING AUTHOR OF *THE HEART OF PERFECTION, MY SISTERS THE SAINTS,* AND *THE NEW FAITHFUL*

"Lila has written a beautiful, must-read book for all of us who feel a calling to right the wrong of this grave injustice called abortion. You will feel compelled to do more, to fight harder, and to dig deep within yourself to sacrifice more of yourself for our most vulnerable in the womb. Read this book—and learn from one of the very best in our movement."

–ABBY JOHNSON, AMERICAN ANTI-ABORTION ACTIVIST

Rose, Lila, 1988-
Fighting for life :
becoming a force for cha
[2021]
33305251279919
sa   06/25/21

FIGHTING
FOR LIFE

BECOMING A FORCE FOR CHANGE
IN A WOUNDED WORLD

LILA ROSE

NELSON
BOOKS
An Imprint of Thomas Nelson

Fighting for Life

© 2021 Lila Rose

All rights reserved. No portion of this book may be reproduced, stored in a retrieval system, or transmitted in any form or by any means—electronic, mechanical, photocopy, recording, scanning, or other—except for brief quotations in critical reviews or articles, without the prior written permission of the publisher.

Published in Nashville, Tennessee, by Nelson Books, an imprint of Thomas Nelson. Nelson Books and Thomas Nelson are registered trademarks of HarperCollins Christian Publishing, Inc.

Published in association with The Bindery Agency, www.TheBinderyAgency.com.

Thomas Nelson titles may be purchased in bulk for educational, business, fundraising, or sales promotional use. For information, please e-mail SpecialMarkets@ThomasNelson.com.

Unless otherwise noted, Scripture quotations taken from The Holy Bible, New International Version˚, NIV˚. Copyright © 1973, 1978, 1984, 2011 by Biblica, Inc.˚ Used by permission of Zondervan. All rights reserved worldwide. www.Zondervan.com. The "NIV" and "New International Version" are trademarks registered in the United States Patent and Trademark Office by Biblica, Inc.˚

Scripture quotations marked AMP are taken from the Amplified˚ Bible (AMP). Copyright © 2015 by The Lockman Foundation. Used by permission. www.lockman.org

Scripture quotations marked ESV are taken from the ESV˚ Bible (The Holy Bible, English Standard Version˚). Copyright © 2001 by Crossway, a publishing ministry of Good News Publishers. Used by permission. All rights reserved.

The Scripture quotations marked NRSVCE are taken from the New Revised Standard Version Bible: Catholic Edition. Copyright © 1989, 1993 National Council of the Churches of Christ in the United States of America. Used by permission. All rights reserved worldwide.

Any internet addresses, phone numbers, or company or product information printed in this book are offered as a resource and are not intended in any way to be or to imply an endorsement by Thomas Nelson, nor does Thomas Nelson vouch for the existence, content, or services of these sites, phone numbers, companies, or products beyond the life of this book.

ISBN 978-1-4002-1987-2 (HC)
ISBN 978-1-4002-1989-6 (audiobook)
ISBN 978-1-4002-1988-9 (eBook)

Library of Congress Control Number: 2021930914

Printed in the United States of America

21 22 23 24 25 LSC 10 9 8 7 6 5 4 3 2 1

To my sister Caterina

Note from the Author

Stories in this book reflect the author's recollection of events. Dialogue has been recreated from memory or transcribed from recordings. Some names and identifying characteristics have been changed to protect the privacy of those depicted.

Contents

PART 3: COMING HOME

Dare to Fight for a Better World

"Bad dream again?" Joe asked.

I nodded. We'd been married only a few months, but this conversation had become something of a morning ritual. Newlywed life in our little apartment in Berkeley, California, was beautiful in so many ways—except for the lack of a dishwasher—and yet, even wedded bliss hadn't stopped the nightmares.

This nightmare was a variation on an old theme. I was back in my parents' house, the house in which I'd grown up. A disaster had just happened or seemed imminent. I was downstairs in our dining room when I heard the weak but piercing cry of an infant. My heart pounding, I raced up the tall staircase toward the sound. Once upstairs, I followed the cries to my old bedroom and rushed in. The shades were drawn and the room was dark.

Where is the crying coming from? I wondered as I frantically searched the room. The sound intensified as I neared the bed. Rummaging through the blankets and pillows, I found nothing. The sound, I realized, was coming from underneath the bed. I fell to my knees on the wooden floor and looked under the bed frame.

There was just enough light to see a shallow gray bucket. Inside the bucket was a naked baby girl, flailing to keep her head above the water and crying desperately. Terrified, I pulled the bucket toward me, the water splashing all around. I picked up the baby and nestled her against my shirt. Cold and trembling, she clung to me, still wailing profusely.

How long has she been here? Where is her mother? I tried to dry her off with my clothes and warm her body with mine, but the more I tried to comfort her, the more she cried. She was inconsolable, as if her ability to be soothed was damaged beyond repair. Somehow I knew she had been left in that bucket to die. At that moment, I felt the abandonment she felt, the total fear that comes with deprivation of human love and touch. *Is this what a child feels when abandoned by her parents?* The dream ended with me holding her in my arms, uncertain what to do next.

I have been having nightmares like this since childhood. In each one, someone—usually a child and sometimes one of my own younger brothers or sisters—is in danger, and I try to help. Always alone, I feel a tremendous sense of responsibility to do something.

In my dreams, the threat is amorphous, vague, uncertain. As I learned at an early age, however, there are evil forces in the world that are tangible and real. They violate the dignity of the human person, especially the vulnerable, and brutalize the most defenseless. As in my dreams, these forces routinely deprive infants of the warmth and love of their mothers, and the damage they do to them is far worse than the worst of my nightmares. The cause to which I've dedicated my life's work has brought me face-to-face with some of these forces, and I've seen evil I can never forget.

I got involved in the pro-life cause as a teenager. Over the next decade, I discovered thousands of others who also wanted to take action to defend the vulnerable. Together we have committed to supporting mothers and fathers in need, educating others about the violence of the abortion industry, and working toward total legal protection for every preborn child.

When I first got involved, I had a strong desire to do something meaningful with my life. Deep down, I think we all want that. I also had a strong sense that I had a responsibility to do something good for the world, to help those in need. Each one of us possesses a conscience and the ability to reason, and we can choose to develop our sense of right and wrong or bury it. But burying it, not doing the work to form our consciences so that we know when to stand up for what is right, is a great poverty that will only bring us unhappiness.

As a Christian, I believe that both our conscience and the responsibility that comes with it is a gift from God. I believe that each of us has the power to choose good but with that freedom we also have the capacity to sin. And this is why the world is so broken.

Our natures are wounded by sin, as Aleksandr Solzhenitsyn said, tearing a line between good and evil "right through every human heart— and through all human hearts."[1]

But we aren't doomed to evil. We can love. We can sacrifice. We can fight for what is right and choose to seek healing for ourselves and the world around us, despite the woundedness. We can dare to make our world better.

Our hearts' response to the needs of the world shapes the causes we take on. What breaks our hearts? What captures our attention? What makes us angry? What brings out the fire in our souls when we see something wrong? These are indicators and starting places. Looking back, I can see how my dreams—or my nightmares—reflect the burden laid on my heart.

Perhaps you can relate. You have a desire to make a difference. Something has captured your attention and aroused your concern. The more you learn about the problem, the more concerned you become. You feel you should do something, but you don't know exactly what or how. If so, I've written this book just for you.

I can't tell you exactly what your path will look like or what your road map for action should be, but I can give you the most important lessons of my own lifelong battle to inspire your tactics and strategies. When we have the right foundations, and when we understand how to grow personally and take action, we can live out our individual callings and help change the world for the better.

This book shares the lessons I have learned in my own work to build one of the world's leading pro-life organizations, Live Action, to grow our movement for justice, and to grow personally. In part 1 are some foundational principles to get you started. It is also the story of the founding of Live Action and the early lessons I learned as a new activist. Part 2 is designed to give you tools to persevere in your mission. In part 3, I share lessons that have helped guide me toward maturity and wholeness in the midst of the battle—lessons that I believe are crucial for all of us.

I am a work in progress: I continue to learn every single day, and, as I'll share throughout this book, to grow each day means we must be willing to make mistakes, to risk ourselves, and to never give up.

The fight for the dignity of all human life—and ultimately, for a world that is more just, more beautiful, and more loving—needs all of us. As I share my story and the lessons I've learned, I hope to encourage and inspire you on your own path to grow, to serve, to defend the weak, and to speak the truth. At times you may feel pressure to be silent, to fit in, to ignore the need you see, and to do what is easier and more comfortable instead. But the world needs *you* to stand up for what is right. It needs your voice, your gifts, your heart. It needs what you uniquely have to offer. Your efforts won't be perfect, but they will be worth it. And by having the courage to stand up, you will inspire others to do the same.

Real change, lasting change, does not come easily and never has. To undo the destruction around us, we have to work to create something new in its place—something good and true and beautiful. Only the balm of goodness can heal the wounds that evil has caused. Only truth can drive out the lies that dehumanize our brothers and sisters. And only beauty can transcend the ugliness that has caused such nightmarish horror.

The world needs men and women of conviction who will not sit by as the battle rages. Let's dare to dream of a world that is better and, together, boldly enter the fray to make it so.

PART 1

GETTING STARTED

CHAPTER 1

Let Your Heart Break

It was a broken heart that first ignited my passion to find my cause.

When I was around nine years old, during afternoon nap time for my younger siblings, my mom flipped on the TV—a rare occurrence in our home and a special treat. A commercial was playing about children in an African nation suffering through a famine. Their bloated bellies, twig-thin legs, and wide, pain-filled eyes called out to me through the screen. The narrator explained that if we acted *now*, if we called the number on the screen and donated just twenty-five dollars a month, we could help save five children from starvation.

Later that week, on a routine trip to the grocery store with my mom, I thought of that commercial. The store was next door to a McDonald's, and it was the time of the Beanie Baby craze of the late 1990s. If you bought a Happy Meal, you got a Teenie Beanie Baby. I noticed that the trash can by the McDonald's was stuffed with Happy Meal boxes, some of which contained still-wrapped hamburgers and cartons full of fries. Customers had bought the Happy Meals for the plush toys and then thrown away the food. I thought of the children I had seen on TV and wondered, *How many children could those Happy Meals have fed?*

This wasn't yet full heartbreak, but it was an awakening. I was hit with the sober reality that every moment, somewhere in the world, a child was starving to death. I sensed that the problem of evil and suffering was inescapable. I was too young to understand it all: human beings torturing each other, children being exploited, brutal regimes exacting cruelty on millions. But I knew enough to see the contrast between my life and the lives of those children. While others endured unimaginable suffering, here I was—privileged, safe and protected.

It was a lot to contemplate as a child, and I was certainly a contemplative and intense nine-year-old. Whether it happens when we're nine or thirty-nine or older, many of us have moments such as these when we are suddenly faced with evil, injustice, and the suffering of the world outside our own. However they happen, these experiences are important. We need to pay attention to them, absorb them, remember them. Such moments of conscience and concern ultimately can become the fuel we need for the long, hard fight that lies ahead. They are also preparation for the heartbreak that can compel us to action.

My sensitivity to the vulnerability of children had a lot to do with my upbringing. My parents loved children and lived with a generosity that extended beyond our family to friends and strangers alike.

Growing up, I was sandwiched between five brothers—two older, three younger. I loved having what seemed like a steady flow of new babies in our home. But as much as I enjoyed my brothers, and all the wrestling and tree climbing that came with them, I desperately wanted a sister. Every night before bed, I knelt by my bed and asked God to give me one.

I was a hopeful little girl, and I felt optimistic about my chances. After all, we had room for another Rose. When I was six, we moved into a bigger house in San Jose. The couple who owned the home were touched by my parents' idealism and passion for family and sold them the home at an under-market price. The empty lot next to the house helped set it apart from the surrounding homes, all the better to protect our neighbors from the bedlam my brothers and I could produce. Although few of my parents' friends could understand why they had so many kids, I continued to hope for one more.

When I was eight, my parents sat down with my five brothers and me to tell us they were expecting another baby. As they did with all the children, Mom and Dad decided to wait until the birth to find out the sex. While we counted down the days until the birth, I eagerly looked again and again at the ten-week ultrasound picture of the baby posted on the refrigerator. I marveled at the fact that a tiny human was growing inside my mother and tried to imagine what my new little sibling would look like.

When labor started for my mom, my parents headed to the hospital and my grandma came over to watch us kids. I waited nervously with my brothers, wondering whether we would be gaining a brother or a sister. I was thrilled when I heard the news. My prayers were answered when Caterina Joy was born.

I immediately fell in love with my baby sister. She was tiny and chubby with wide blue eyes and soft skin. I cuddled her for hours, amazed that a whole person was contained in her little body. Two years later, my parents had their eighth and last child, Nina, another beautiful little girl.

It was in the midst of all this love and chaos that I experienced my first life-changing heartbreak. Given my parents' passion for classical education, our house was always full of books. Ignoring house rules, I would turn up the thermostat, grab a blanket, and head to the floor vent behind the couch where I could cocoon in my heat bubble. Secluding myself out of my mom's line of sight lessened the odds I'd be recruited for chores. Hidden behind the sofa, I'd read for hours: Nancy Drew, the Chronicles of Narnia, *Little Women*, the Little House books of Laura Ingalls Wilder, and more.

One afternoon, I pulled from a lower shelf a small paperback creased from wear and tear and gray with age. On the front cover was an image of a sober-looking woman under the title, *A Handbook on Abortion*. The book was written by Dr. and Mrs. J. C. Willke, founders of National Right to Life. Inside were pictures.

I was not prepared for the images I saw in that book. Shocked and horrified, I quickly shut the book and sat back. *What did I just see?* Feeling

I was on the brink of an important discovery, I opened up the book again. I was staring at the photo of a tiny baby with tiny arms and legs severed from a tiny body. I was looking at a little human being during the first trimester torn into pieces by a powerful suction abortion. Heartbroken, I remembered my baby sister's ultrasound photo. *Is this real? How could anyone do this to a baby?*

I wanted to learn more. I knew my parents were subscribers to the *National Right to Life* newsletter. Digging around the house, I found a recent copy. The newsletter included diagrams that showed the four stages of a D&X abortion, short for "dilation and extraction," sometimes called a "partial birth abortion." The procedure was being hotly debated: Twice, a Republican-controlled Congress sent a bill to President Bill Clinton to authorize a ban. Twice, Clinton vetoed the legislation.[1]

I looked at the diagrams in horror. They showed a fully formed infant delivered feet first, up to his neck. With the baby's legs dangling and kicking and his head still in the birth canal, the doctor pierced his neck with scissors and then placed a suction tube inside his skull. With his brain sucked out, his skull collapsed, and he was pulled out of the birth canal dead.

Even the pro-abortion groups admitted this procedure was committed at least five hundred times a year. I was still a child myself, but I was old enough to wonder how we could possibly allow an atrocity like this to take place just about every day—not in some place oceans away, but right here in America, in California, in clinics just miles from where I lived.

I continued reading. There were more than a million abortions in the United States every year. *One million.* Many of those children were smaller, less developed than the baby I was looking at in the diagram, but each one was a human being. With a mother. With a father. Maybe with a big sister or brother. It broke my heart to keep reading but keep reading I did.

It was hard for me to believe that abortion was legal. Even harder to believe was that everyday people, who might be my neighbors or members of my community, agreed that it should be legal, as did almost all the major media outlets. The *Los Angeles Times* said abortion supporters actually "cheered" the decision to keep partial birth abortion legal.[2] I didn't know what to do with this information or even what it meant, but I knew there was evil in the world. I sensed my life would never be the same.

It is heart-wrenching to even think about such things. It hurts to open our hearts. It's easier to look away from the suffering and injustice in the world and pretend they do not exist, or, if they do exist, to pretend we have no role in addressing them. But heartbreak in the face of suffering and injustice is necessary. It is the natural response to seeing harm done, especially to the innocent. It reminds us we have the ability to love, a precious but painful gift that God has given us.

Heartbreak comes easily to children. Children respond to love with wholehearted love and to evil and wrongdoing with sorrow and fear. We are more innocent as children and have had less time to do evil ourselves. Being less jaded and more open, our souls naturally respond with concern when we see someone hurt or mistreated. It is no wonder Jesus said that "unless you change and become like little children, you will never enter the kingdom of heaven" (Matthew 18:3).

Looking back, I realize what a gift it was to experience heartbreak over the evil of abortion as a child. It gave me the drive to start my organization, Live Action, at a young age. It deepened my empathy and inspired me to direct my energy away from myself and my own interests and toward the most vulnerable. Without heartbreak, it would have been easy to do some good work and live a normal life, leaving the fight to others. It would have been easier still to shut down and ignore injustice and tragedy altogether. But by avoiding the risk of hurting, I would have limited my own ability to serve. Allowing our hearts to remain broken for people in danger, especially the most vulnerable, is a necessary pain.

Meaningful social action almost inevitably begins with heartbreak. Social action requires vulnerability, the willingness to let down our guard and allow ourselves to be wounded and even scarred by evil so we can find the passion we need to confront it.

As adults we may need to recognize and dismantle the self-protective mechanisms we use to ward off heartbreak. We may need to let go of judgments or cynicism that allow us to justify the suffering of others. We may need to enter into another person's need or suffering rather than numbing our sorrow or anger over tragedy. We may need to look beyond the routine distractions of daily life, including the pursuit of our own comfort or interests, so that our hearts can be broken by the pain of those in need.

Deep grief is often the starting point for righting an injustice. And that's a good thing. Don't run away from that emotion. Sit with it, let it break you open, let it move you. Don't suppress it. The world has enough hearts of stone. It needs hearts willing to ache and burn. Grief, as well as the healthy anger that often accompanies it, can fuel your passion to fight a seemingly impossible fight.

The good news is that we aren't alone in allowing our hearts to be broken in this way. As a Christian, I believe that God became a man in the person of Jesus, and that by doing so and taking on our human nature, he allowed his own heart to break over the wounds and sin of all humanity. Whatever grief you and I might feel, we are in good company because Jesus has experienced it all. In the Gospels, he set the ultimate example of perfect compassion. Jesus wept, he mourned, and he endured great agony as he prepared to give up his life for the redemption of all humanity. Part of his agony was knowing he would be rejected by many of those whom he came to love and save. Jesus Christ, tortured and wounded, dying on a cross with nails in his hands and feet, took on all the heartbreak in the world. And he invites us to unite our love to his, to draw on his strength, and to allow our hearts to break with his.

CHAPTER 2

Find Your Heroes

From the time I could read, my mom and I belonged to a mother-daughter book club. If I ever have a daughter, I hope to do the same with her. The book club was an amazing way to learn and to build friendships with other families, not to mention spend quality time with my mom.

Each month we read a particular book and then met with other mothers and daughters to discuss it. The mother and daughter whose turn it was to host made dinner, set a formal table, and prepared discussion questions. One of the first books we read was *The Hiding Place*, the true story of Corrie ten Boom and her sister, Betsie, two seemingly ordinary Dutch women who lived extraordinary lives during the Second World War. This book had a powerful influence on me. These sisters showed me what true heroism is and how courageous love is possible in the face of great evil.

The Hiding Place told of the horrors inflicted on Jews and those who dared to help them. Just as important, the book spoke to the power of God's light in some of history's darkest corners. Corrie and Betsie lived with their elderly father, Casper, above his watch repair shop in Amsterdam during the Nazi occupation. As persecution of the Jews intensified, this little Christian family joined the underground and volunteered to hide Jews in their home.

Eventually, a Dutch informant betrayed the ten Booms to the German state police, the Gestapo, and they promptly arrested the entire family. Sent to a concentration camp in Germany, Betsie and Corrie endured terrible deprivation and cruelty, but they never lost their faith in God's love and mercy. Despite the beatings, the starvation, and the grueling forced labor, the sisters joyfully shared their love of God with everyone around them. Defying the risk, they hid away a Bible to teach the other prisoners about Jesus.

Casper had been separated from the girls after his arrest and incarcerated elsewhere. While still imprisoned, the sisters learned of their father's death and burial in an unmarked grave. Filled with fury toward those responsible for her father's death, Corrie prayed to God for the power to forgive the informant who had betrayed them. Years later, she wrote, "I discovered that it is not on our forgiveness any more than on our goodness that the world's healing hinges, but on his. When he tells us to love our enemies, he gives, along with the command, the love itself."[1]

Betsie broke physically under the strain but never spiritually. As she was dying, she said to Corrie, "We must tell people what we have learned here. We must tell them that there is no pit so deep that he is not deeper still. They will listen to us, Corrie, because we have been here."[2] Miraculously, Corrie was freed soon after Betsie's death. She would eventually open a home to help rehabilitate those imprisoned and tortured by the Nazis, and there, among those broken people, she would share the good news of eternal life.

Years later, I learned the story of another Holocaust victim who was able to love in the face of great horror. A priest serving in Poland when the Nazis invaded, Father Maximilian Kolbe had risked his life sheltering Jews. Eventually, the Gestapo arrested him and sent him to the infamous death camp, Auschwitz. Once, when a camp prisoner went missing, the camp commander ordered a roll call and selected ten men at random for a unique torture.

To deter future escapes, the commander condemned the men to an underground bunker where they would slowly die of thirst and hunger.

On being selected, one of the men cried out, "My wife! My children!" Overwhelmed with compassion for the man, Father Kolbe asked to be taken in the man's place, and the commander obliged.[3]

Kolbe spent his time in the bunker leading the other men in prayer and song. When Kolbe still had not died after three weeks without food and water, camp guards injected him with carbolic acid. Witnesses say his face was full of peace and joy as he left this world.

Where does the strength come from to risk or even offer one's life for another, especially a stranger? Only love—the choice to affirm and will the good of the other—can motivate one person to die for another. The ability to love like this is given to us by God. Father Kolbe and the ten Booms personally drew their strength from the self-sacrificing love of Jesus Christ. When I read about their lives, I wanted to be able to love like that, to love heroically. My heroes showed me a source for strength far greater than myself.

In addition to reading about heroes in book club, I discovered even more heroes in childhood during trips with my dad to a nearby Catholic bookstore. We weren't Catholic growing up but, as an educator and lover of books, my dad took seriously C. S. Lewis's admonition to read at least one "old book" for every new book.[4] And the Catholic bookstore was full of old books.

In my dad's beat-up white Dodge sedan, we drove the twenty-minute trip to the strip mall where the store was located. The parking lot always had plenty of open spaces, not a good sign for the mall's humble businesses. The bookstore's modest front included a blue curtain overlay at the top of the windows that was printed with words in white capital letters: ROSARIES. JEWELRY. CANDLES. BOOKS. CLERGY APPAREL. CARDS. GIFTS.

I was about eleven the first time Dad took me along. Stepping inside onto the old low-pile carpet, I looked around in wonder. As a lover of trinkets, I felt as if I had just entered a religious Disneyland. Pillars with little glass doors were set along the shopper's path with medals and bracelets and confirmation gifts. Against the back wall, looping around the store, were rows and rows of bookcases.

As we slowly made our way to the shelves, I got distracted by the icons set out in display cases. The images that captivated me most were those of Mary holding Jesus as a baby. Although all Christians—and Muslims as well—respect Mary as the mother of Jesus, I never heard much about Mary in my church growing up except at Christmastime when we sang songs such as "Mary, Did You Know?" Occasionally, our pastor reminded us that Mary was an ordinary young girl, just like anyone else, and God chose her to be the mother of Jesus.

Mary did not seem so ordinary to me. An angel had appeared to her, telling her she was "full of grace" and that she would bear the Son of God. Given the burdens the birth of a child would mean for her, Mary could have protested. Unmarried and pregnant, she risked certain scorn and possible exile from her own community. Instead, Mary answered the angel, "Behold, I am the servant of the Lord; may it be done to me according to your word" (Luke 1:38 AMP).

And there was Joseph, her betrothed. The Gospels tell us in some detail the natural confusion he faced in light of a pregnancy for which he was not responsible. It was an angel that convinced him: "do not be afraid to take Mary home as your wife, because what is conceived in her is from the Holy Spirit" (Matthew 1:20). Quiet and faithful, Joseph's entire life became focused on protecting and caring for Mary and Jesus.

I also wondered what Mary looked like, how she behaved, how she loved. During one visit to the Catholic bookstore, a particular icon captured my attention. It was small, about the size of my hand. A rich turquoise color framed the edges. Mary was wearing a deep red robe and head covering, and Jesus was nestled in her arms, peaceful and safe. Her dark eyes looked out with intensity, and I marveled at how she seemed strong but gentle, brave but still vulnerable. Even though at peace, she also looked a little sad. It was as if she knew, even as she held her perfect baby, that there would be tremendous suffering to come.

A "righteous and devout" man named Simeon told a young Mary with her newborn that "a sword will pierce your own soul too" (Luke 2:25, 35). She would feel some of the suffering her Son would endure to save humanity. Her heart was open to be broken but, drawing on the most powerful source in the world, the love of God, she would choose to stay with her Son at the cross as he took his last breaths.

The icon was twenty dollars, but I convinced my dad to buy it for me. I kept it in my room on a little shelf next to my bed so I could look at it as I fell asleep. A desire began forming in my heart to *be* like Mary. Loving. Brave. Willing to say yes to a little baby, totally unexpected. Willing to risk everything to love him even though she sensed in her heart the great horror he would one day endure. Willing, finally, to stand at the foot of the cross, risking death when nearly everyone else had fled.

It was in that same bookstore that I discovered yet another hero. At the back of the store were the old books that told of saints who had lived and died in the name of Christ going back two millennia. As I browsed the bookshelves, the image of another woman caught my attention. An international icon of charity at the time of her death just a few years earlier, Mother Teresa was also a champion of life. I had come across pro-life quotes of hers on the Internet while researching abortion, and I was excited to find that the store sold compilations of her writings and talks.

I bought two books. One, *Loving Jesus*, showed Mother Teresa looking wrinkled, wise, and compassionate. The second, *Total Surrender*, showed Mother Teresa looking more serious, even severe. I would learn that Mother Teresa felt great joy and peace at the beginning of her ministry, but later she experienced great internal suffering. She faced doubts and endured an experience of spiritual desolation, but even during her trials she chose to trust God, no matter how difficult the choice.

As a young girl, Mother Teresa, whose name was Agnes Bojaxhiu, heard God's voice and listened, rising from a little town in the Balkans to become a force for good throughout the world. She took to heart Jesus' teaching that loving the "least of these" was loving Jesus himself. She went out into the streets of Calcutta, India, and found the most destitute in order to love them as she loved Jesus himself. Every person she encountered was Jesus to her.

Mother Teresa was not beautiful by the world's standards, but she possessed a powerful radiance that inspired millions of every creed and nation. She was a tiny nun who wore a simple white sari and spent most of her time in the slums of Calcutta. The unbelievable poverty and human suffering that surrounded Mother Teresa only inspired her and her fellow sisters to treat all of humanity as children of God.

Her writing shifted the way I saw the world. She was teaching me the same lesson she taught the world throughout her life: to treat every single person as precious and worth fighting for. She opened my eyes to seeing each person as Jesus himself might have seen him or her, as unique, as holy, as made in God's image. That's the power of a hero—to change our understanding of the world, to challenge us to greater love.

Mother Teresa taught me that there is no excuse for failing to love not just my friends and family but also the cashier at the grocery store or the person passing me on the street. She revered the helpless child in the womb as Jesus in disguise, and she urged every mother, no matter the difficulty, to embrace life. It struck me deeply that of all the evils in the world—poverty, war, hunger—it was abortion that Mother Teresa considered "the greatest destroyer of love and peace."[5] Even more impressive, Mother Teresa had the courage to say this at the National Prayer Breakfast with President Clinton and other powerful abortion supporters in the room.

At the same event, she also said, "If we accept that a mother can kill her own child, how can we tell other people not to kill one another?"[6] She made it clear that no matter how wealthy or privileged or free the United States might be, by accepting abortion, we were sowing violence where there should be peace and harmony. She taught that the greatest poverty was spiritual poverty—the rejection of God and others, and, especially, saying no to the life of a child. True wealth, by contrast, was not to be found in material things but in recognizing God himself in the face of every person we encounter.

I have a close friend who witnessed this kind of true wealth when she served with the religious congregation Mother Teresa founded, the Missionaries of Charity in Calcutta. At first my friend was overwhelmed by her work as a volunteer to help the nurses in the clinic for the dying. She was shocked at the raw suffering of so many people dying in the streets. She recalled in particular the case of a woman sold as a sexual slave who had been left by a sewer to die.

When the woman was brought into the clinic, her open sores were covered in maggots. Although this woman had known only deprivation and suffering in her life, the sisters cleaned every open sore and carefully sutured each wound as lovingly as if she were their own mother. She had been subjected to conditions that violated her God-given dignity, but in the woman's dying days Mother Teresa's sisters fought to restore it. They demonstrated that, for all the abuse her heart and body had endured, her dignity as a daughter of God could never be destroyed.

The harshness of life in Calcutta's slums had etched deep wrinkles in Mother Teresa's face and left her sandaled feet calloused and twisted. When I was a teen, I found a photograph of her gnarled feet and kept it in my bedroom to remind me what true beauty looked like. Her wrinkled face, her twisted feet—these exuded beauty to me. Hers was a supernatural beauty that poured out from her heart and soul. Mother Teresa became my hero.

What I learned from reading about Mother Teresa was much the same lesson I learned from reading about Corrie and Betsie ten Boom and Father Kolbe: heroism is grounded in self-sacrificing love. Instead of taking life or leaving those in danger to suffer alone, heroes offer up their lives for others, even to the point of death.

As we take our first steps to make a difference in the world, it helps to ask ourselves, Who are my heroes? Whom do I aspire to emulate? Who inspires me enough to read their works, to watch their talks, to follow them on social media? We may not realize that they are influencing us, but they likely are. In choosing whom to learn from and follow, we have to ask some additional questions: Do the people I admire live for themselves—for their own glory, wealth, pleasure, and successes—or do they live for others? Do they look to themselves as their source of truth, love, and salvation, or do they look to God?

Stories move us in ways arguments and theories cannot. In ways we may not even notice, the stories of others rework the way we see the world. The stories of true heroes remind us of what is good in this world, and they inspire us to strive for good ourselves. We have to choose our heroes carefully. Inevitably, we will emulate those we admire.

We are each created to live out a heroic love in a world desperately in need of it. If we choose to follow any other path—taking shortcuts on love or detouring around the opportunity to do good—we reject the greatness for which we are made.

Choose your heroes intentionally and wisely. Study their lives, read their words, put into daily action their call to love others with the love of God. As the ten Booms, Father Kolbe, Mary, and Mother Teresa could attest, heroic love requires not merely our best but our all. It is only by saying yes to heroic love, with all the pain and the risk it can involve, that we become the people we were created to be. With heroic examples in our hearts, may we discover the inspiration to do the same.

CHAPTER 3

Know Your Gifts

As a young girl, my mother often told me I could accomplish anything I put my mind to. A big dreamer, she enthusiastically encouraged my siblings and me to explore things that interested us and to experiment. My mom's affirmation gave me confidence to try new things and not to be afraid of failure.

My dad's mother, Grandma Judy, was always volunteering for good causes. She knitted hundreds of little blankets for children in a Romanian orphanage and other children in need. She routinely sent money, even if just a few dollars a month, to scores of nonprofits, and she helped out at the local community pregnancy center. She loved including her grand-kids in her volunteer work.

One day, she invited me to help her at the pregnancy center, and she and I spent an afternoon stuffing envelopes for an upcoming fundraiser, the center's annual Walk for Life. With the money raised from the event, the center could buy an ultrasound machine so women in need could see their babies before they were born. Having five younger siblings, I had seen my share of ultrasound pictures posted on our refrigerator. Those pictures were always exciting to me, and I could only imagine how exciting they would be to new moms and dads.

The pregnancy center encouraged families to raise money in advance by securing sponsors for their walk around the park. Although only nine, I was captivated by the idea that I could actually help mothers and children. All I had to do was ask! I spent a whole month pestering every adult I came in contact with to sponsor me. I also spent hours on the phone calling friends and family. I even cold-called people whose names I found in the church directory. I did not know at the time that soliciting was against church policy, but thankfully, our church was a generous one, and most people I approached had a soft spot for a nine-year-old passionate about mothers and babies. It felt exhilarating, being able to help others in such a tangible way, even though I was only a kid. I ended up raising more than $3,000. Better still, my dad had promised to match whatever I raised.

We went to the walk as a family, and I helped my mom push my baby brother around the park in the stroller. I practically skipped with pride, happy that I was able to help my mom and the center. At the program after the walk, one of the organizers announced the center had raised enough money to buy an ultrasound machine. Then they shared who the top fundraisers were in categories based on age and how much they had each raised. As they moved through each category, I learned that I had out-raised the child, teen, and young-adult top fundraisers combined. Better still, it had been fun!

The walk became a turning point in my young life. I had no idea how much difference I could make simply by recruiting people around me to support the center, and it wasn't *that* hard to ask once I got started. In the process, I learned that I had a gift for taking the initiative and rallying other people to help.

Think back to a moment in your life when you felt most alive in the work you were doing. That experience of aliveness is key to discovering not only your passion but also your gifts. Maybe you already know the gifts you have or are working to develop your skills. Or maybe you're still wondering what your particular gifts and talents might be. Start with what brings you life—things you enjoy and things you are naturally good at. What do people praise you for? What do the people closest to you, the people you trust, see as your strengths? What activity so engrosses you that you lose all sense of time?

God gave you your strengths for a reason. When you fight for a cause, you put your unique gifts to work for him and for humanity. You are unrepeatable, both biologically and spiritually. Among the billions of people who inhabit this planet, there is no one exactly like you. Even if you had an identical twin, with the same DNA, who was raised under the same roof as you, you each would have different personalities, interests, and gifts.

These differences are obvious: some of us find math easy; others find it difficult. Some of us are extroverted, others introverted. Some of us are long-term planners, and others like to live by the seat of our pants. Is this all random chance? No. God designed us with unique and individual sets of talents and gifts for a reason. They are given to us to be used and developed so we can better serve others.

Several years after the Walk for Life, when I was a student at UCLA, I learned another valuable lesson about our individual gifts—specifically, about the dangers of comparing gifts. I had gone with some friends to a Bible study held in a top-floor apartment near Hollywood. It was upscale without being pretentious, the kind of place in which I imagined a lot of aspiring actors, musicians, and creators lived.

Once inside the apartment, I found a place on the couch. An animated twentysomething man named Jamil was talking about how hard it was to be a Christian musician in Los Angeles. He was good enough to have once worked on a project with a famous rapper and producer, but his refusal to compromise on the lyrics he wrote had limited his own progress as a performer. He shared how he had watched other rappers he had worked with gain fame and success while his own career seemed to stall.

"But God told me it was okay," he said. "God told me, 'Jamil, you have to stay in your lane. Stop looking at what I am doing in other people's lives or what the Evil One may be doing in other people's lives. Look at your own life and what I am calling you to do. If you start to look over at other people in their lanes, you will crash!'" Jamil had a gift for music. Despite the temptation to use his gift in a way that compromised his values, he understood that God had given him that gift for a purpose—to create music that honored God. Jamil did just that.

Since the beginning of time, people have coveted the gifts and possessions of others. In Genesis, we learn that brothers Cain and Abel each presented God an offering: Cain presented fruit from the ground, and Abel presented a sheep from his flock. God preferred Abel's gift, and Cain went off sulking. God said to Cain, "Why are you angry, and why has your countenance fallen? If you do well, will you not be accepted? And if you do not do well, sin is lurking at the door; its desire is for you, but you must master it" (Genesis 4:6–7 NRSVCE). And yet, instead of trusting that if he did his best God would give him what he needed, Cain killed Abel in a fit of jealousy.

It's no accident that two of the Ten Commandments deal with envy. "You shall not commit adultery. . . . You shall not covet your neighbor's house; you shall not covet your neighbor's wife," God told Moses and added, "or anything that belongs to your neighbor" (Exodus 20:14, 17 NRSVCE).

We can admire the gifts and talents of others and look to them for inspiration, but once we begin to covet what they have, we lose our way. Comparing ourselves to others inevitably makes us feel inferior or, just as bad, brings us to self-satisfied feelings of superiority. Constant comparisons also limit our ability to focus on our own unique talents and gifts, what we can do to serve others, what we are called to do, and how we can grow to become the best people we can be.

It can be easy to adopt a scarcity mentality about our own gifts and abilities; we think that if someone else is using their gifts and making an impact, then somehow our gifts and the impact they can make are less valuable. This competitive mindset only cripples us, causing us to perceive others as threats instead of allies. Instead, we should think collaboratively. God created our diversity of talents, abilities, and experiences so that we can work and serve better together. The differences we have with others are by design, not accident. We can appreciate and celebrate the gifts and successes of others, then focus on using the gifts and graces we've been given.

Unfortunately, many of the technologies we use and much of the media we consume only breeds comparison and competition. Social media apps are designed to make us seek influence and more popularity with others and to compare ourselves when we don't get as many likes or shares or comments. Media is full of images of aspirational lifestyles, airbrushed bodies and faces, clothes, vacations, even idealized relationships that can tempt us to envy or compare. It shouldn't surprise us that most social media users feel worse about themselves after using an app, not better. But I'd encourage you not to miss your own life by becoming absorbed in someone else's. God has gifts he has entrusted to you specifically, and the purpose of those abilities and graces is to use them in service of others. Don't waste your precious time comparing your life to another's. Instead, glean whatever lessons, whatever inspiration, you can from others, and then use the gifts and graces you've been given to serve the world.

If Jamil had wasted all his focus and energy on wishing for the success other artists had instead of developing his own gifts in service of others, he would have wasted his God-given potential. Instead, he chose to be heavily involved in his church and to excel in his musical abilities in a way that honored God. The solution to envy and comparison is twofold: *focus* on what you've set out to do with the talents and abilities God gave you, then *trust* that God will help you make the best of the gifts you've been given.

We step into our creative power when we acknowledge and embrace the gifts we have been given. Our gifts are the weapons needed to change the world.

CHAPTER 4

Know Your Worth

Next to the house I grew up in was a vacant lot filled with waist-high weeds and wildflowers. As a teen, I sometimes went there to be alone and to settle my mind when things in the house felt too chaotic. This time, I went on my own special mission. I had a small pocketknife that my dad had given me as a stocking stuffer a few Christmases back when I was twelve. Thinking little of it at the time, I put it in a bathroom drawer along with random nail polishes, ever-elusive hair ties, and other odds and ends. But over the last few months, I'd found a purpose for that knife, one that soon secretly consumed me.

During my worst moments, I had locked myself in the bathroom and used the knife to make shallow cuts in my skin. I knew cutting myself was wrong, but I felt desperate. Negative voices had been ringing in my head and telling me I was worthless, that there was no point to anything. Looking back now, I understand I was using the knife to create some kind of release for the overwhelming numbness and pain I felt inside. For similar reasons, I sometimes ate little to nothing for days or binged and then purged. Cutting and extreme behaviors with food were the experimental coping strategies I had developed for dealing with a depression that had descended on me over the previous year like a bewildering fog. Feeling paralyzed, I would spend hours curled into a ball in my bedroom, unable to move.

Though I didn't understand it in the midst of the pain, after years of prayer, reflection, and counseling, I can now see some of the pressure points and wounds that contributed to my downward spiral. Deeply sensitive and prone to perfectionism, I was already wrestling with the normal changes that girls experience in adolescence while trying to excel in everything I did. In many ways I was high-functioning, and I could hide much of the inner turmoil. But these fairly typical stresses were exacerbated by problems that had existed in our family since before I was born: problems that included a history of mental health issues on both sides of our family. In particular, my dad's mental health struggles, which had gone undiagnosed and untreated for years, and my mother's lack of resources needed to cope with it.

As could be expected, even with my parents' hard work, goodwill, and idealism, these struggles left their mark on us kids. It also did not help that there was a growing trend among young teens to experiment with self-harm, and when I first heard about the concept of cutting, in pain and desperation, I began to experiment too.

When ideas of throwing myself off our upstairs balcony pushed their way into my mind, I told a close friend, who urged me to tell my parents about what I was experiencing and get help.

I had come to the field that day to bury the knife. It was my own small way of marking a fresh start—the beginning pursuit of healing I knew I desperately needed. Soon after that, I opened up to my parents about the secret binging and purging, the anger and pain that lingered inside of me, the self-loathing that weighed on me like a boulder. They had recently started going to counseling themselves for the first time in their lives, and they were eager for me to have the help I needed too. I started going to counseling, got on medication, and tried to leave the darkest moments behind in hopes of seeking something brighter. I had felt like dying, but I knew that death would not stop the pain. I knew that my life was not mine to take. Despite the psychological emptiness, deep in my soul I knew life was worth living, and that there were oceans of meaning in my life. I just needed to learn how to live again.

Viktor Frankl, the Holocaust survivor and psychiatrist who wrote the masterpiece *Man's Search for Meaning*, told the story of two men in a concentration camp. Both men were contemplating suicide, but Dr. Frankl was able to counsel them out of their despair. He did so by reminding the men that the inhuman conditions of the camp could not deprive them of one essential element: meaning.

For one man, meaning came from remembering his son who lived safely in a foreign country. For the other man, meaning came from the hope he might yet have a promising future as a scientist. Frankl wrote, "A man who becomes conscious of the responsibility he bears toward a human being who affectionately waits for him, or to an unfinished work, will never be able to throw away his life. He knows the 'why' for his existence, and will be able to bear almost any 'how.'"[1]

Although I did not know of Frankl's work at the time, part of what gave me the courage to bury that pocketknife was the meaning I was beginning to find in my pro-life work with Live Action. I was at a stage in my faith when I was struggling with doubts, but there was a cause stirring inside of me. Seeing the need in the world around me helped me take my eyes off my own pain. Even when I felt the most lifeless and hopeless, this cause gave my life purpose.

If I believed life was precious, if I believed human beings had dignity, I had to extend those beliefs to my own person. I knew enough to ask myself, *How can I care about other people's lives if I do not care for my own?* I could not keep harming myself as I had been. Even when I didn't feel it or when I doubted it, I had to hope that God loved me and had a plan for my life.

Many of us have a private struggle with our own self-worth. We wonder if we are loved. Many of us come from families that have a tremendous amount of beauty and good but that also carry wounds. The struggles will manifest themselves differently for each person. Some of us may have a "knife," something we do that harms us, a bad habit, a way we mistreat ourselves. Self-harm can take the form of an addiction—to pornography, video games, shopping, or social media. Self-harm can also take the form of an obsessive comparison of ourselves to others, a habit of negative self-talk, or the repetition of behaviors that we know are not good for us but we feel compelled to do anyway.

Believing that our lives have meaning, as Viktor Frankl said, is a necessary first step out of that destructive place, but it is not sufficient. To resolve our struggle with worth, it is crucial that we understand what it means to be human and where our worth comes from. Human beings are not just components of a larger political structure. We are not just cogs in the wheel of an economy. We are not just subjects to be controlled by mass bureaucracies. All humans possess intrinsic human dignity. That dignity is not dependent on our qualities, on our virtue or lack thereof, on our failures or successes, on what society thinks of us or how the law treats us. Our dignity comes from our Creator, who made us in his image and who created us for eternal life with him, which is the deepest desire of the human soul.

Every human being is loved as a unique individual by a personal God, and we each have the freedom to love him and others as well. What does that love mean? It means that God delights in our existence and wills good for us, even to the point of dying for us.

The German philosopher Josef Pieper wrote that true love affirms the loved one's very existence: "It's good that you exist; it's good that you are in this world!" Pieper went on to describe love as "a mode of willing."[2] Thirteenth-century philosopher and theologian Thomas Aquinas wrote, "To love is to will the good of the other."[3] In other words, love is a choice, an act of the will, for the good of the other person. The ultimate expression of love, as Jesus Christ himself said, is this: "Greater love has no one than this: to lay down one's life for one's friends" (John 15:13).

We cannot love our neighbor as ourselves if we do not first see ourselves as worth loving. Accepting that we are worthy of love is not selfishness, nor is it self-worship. It is preparation for the battle ahead. If we are going to fight for a cause, especially one that could alienate many of those around us, our sense of worth may be called into question, either by external enemies or by internal doubts. To push through, we have to learn to see ourselves the way God sees us—as creatures who are unconditionally loved by him and, through baptism, as daughters and sons. We must consciously reject the lies about our worth that may come from our childhood, the world around us, or an inexplicable voice inside of us. Once we reject these lies, we replace them with this truth: to be human is to be precious in the eyes of God. Each of us is made in His image, loved by Him, and given the power to love.

If our work to change the world is rooted in our belovedness, we can face any challenge, endure any persecution, and overcome any resistance. We can bring His love to others. "For God so loved the world" (John 3:16).

CHAPTER 5

Let God Find You

I had a lot of odd jobs growing up, from scrubbing our neighbor's toilets to babysitting, to tutoring. When I was sixteen and old enough, I applied to a number of stores near our local shopping center. My dream job was working at Safeway and, because I was too young to be a cashier, Safeway hired me as a bagger. (After a few months, I found an opening at the café across the street and discovered I liked being a hostess and a waitress even more.)

As a bagger, I loved talking with customers amid the hustle and bustle of the checkout line. I can't say that I was the best bagger, but I tried to be a friendly one, and my clients generously overlooked their disorganized shopping bags.

If it was slow at the front of the store, I would wander through the aisles and offer to help customers with questions or check on displays. My coworker Kevin worked most late afternoons and evenings in the produce section stocking vegetables. Occasionally we would discuss poetry or books since we were avid readers. At this point, I had been in counseling for several months and had already started taking medication, but I was still wrestling with what it meant to believe in Christ and be a Christian. I was going through a questioning phase of faith, but Kevin was a newfound Christian and was very studious in his desire to seek God.

"I know Jesus existed two thousand years ago in person, but how do I experience him today? How do I find him?" I asked.

"It's good to keep looking for him," Kevin said. "But remember, more than you are looking for him, he's looking for you."

The next day at work Kevin had printed something out for me, a poem by English writer Francis Thompson called "The Hound of Heaven." It begins:

> I fled Him, down the nights and down the days;
> I fled Him, down the arches of the years;
> I fled Him down the labyrinthine ways
> Of my own mind and in the mist of tears . . .[1]

The poet went on to explain that, despite his best efforts, God still loved him and ultimately found him: "Rise, clasp My hand, and come!" I didn't realize it then, but those words would come back to me in all their vivid imagery when I rediscovered my childhood faith over the next few years. I thought I had set out to find God, but now I could see that all along he was finding me.

God is always searching for us. He is always inviting us to see him, to see the world and ourselves in the light of faith in him, to enter into the deeper currents beneath our everyday experience. But God does not force himself on us. Out of love, he gives us the freedom to choose to acknowledge him or not, to receive him or not.

No matter how much I thought that I was the one seeking God, all of my life God was actually seeking me. And the cause I would "find"? No, it was he who gave it to me. Though I didn't see it at the time, he was with me in my darkest moments. He had been the source of my hope. Despite the reality of evil in the world, I knew there was goodness and that he offered himself as the ultimate good. I saw him in the faces of my little siblings. I saw him in the beauty of the star-studded sky in my backyard at night.

Some say that faith is unreasonable and blind, that believing in a God who created the world is like believing in a magical genie. But I think it's more unreasonable to believe that this beautiful, extraordinarily complex world, populated by billions of uniquely designed human beings, is an accident, the result of total chance. I think it requires a suspension of reason to argue that life on Earth somehow started on its own. Scientists are no closer today than they were a century ago to establishing even a halfway plausible theory as to how life on Earth might have begun without God.

Some scientists are confident they know how the universe started, but the prevailing theory, the Big Bang, begs the question of who or what generated that initial explosion. One of the laws of physics states that all matter comes from somewhere. It seems more reasonable to believe that an intelligent God set matter in motion than to believe that matter, with perhaps a sprinkling of fairy dust, somehow unleashed itself. According to philosopher Blaise Pascal's wager, the right "bet" was to believe God was good, loving, and all-powerful. Forget faith for a moment. Reason argues for a First Cause. On every level, I was and remain convinced of this truth.

Since I was a little girl, I have felt drawn to the truth of God's existence. I have had the belief that there is an all-powerful God who loves me and has a plan for me. This belief made me want to understand what that plan was. As I got older, I found myself doubting whether this God existed, whether I had value, and whether there really was a plan for my life.

Still, deep down, I had hope that God had a specific purpose just for me, and I had a sense that the plan went beyond living a normal, quiet, white-picket-fence kind of life. I wanted my life to mean something. I wanted to help those around me and make a difference in the world. As I learned more and more about abortion and all its attendant problems, I asked God to find me. "God, use me," I prayed. "Use me to somehow save lives."

I knew that for my faith to mean anything I needed to make it the top priority of my life. If I was really going to follow Christ, I would have to honor his commandments and strive to be like him. My ultimate cause would be to share his gospel, the good news that in Christ there is salvation from sin and victory over death. This wasn't something I could do on weekends or as a side job. Following Christ had to take over my entire life. Any work I did had to be in service to him. The God I was trying to follow had endured the worst imaginable suffering and laid down his life in order to love me. Now, he was calling on me to pick up my cross and follow him.

We are all in different places on our journeys with God. Maybe you wrestle with whether or not you believe God exists, maybe you are still figuring out who God is, or maybe you have committed yourself to Christ. After I committed to follow Christ, I came to realize it had to change everything about the way I lived. God was not just the source of strength to live out my purpose and fight for my cause. To love and know God must *be* my ultimate purpose and cause.

However important our chosen causes might be, we should ask ourselves, What is our ultimate goal? I realized early in my journey of faith that my end goal should not be to change myself or even change the world. Yes, these goals have value because they serve our final purpose: to live forever in union with God in heaven, and, by sharing the gospel, to bring as many souls as possible with us. And that ugly thing called suffering, that ever-present reality called evil, and, yes, even death itself—each would be forever vanquished by the all-powerful God we serve.

CHAPTER 6

Find Your Cause

In 1963, Jewish philosopher and writer Hannah Arendt, who had fled Germany as Hitler came to power, coined the phrase "banality of evil" in her reporting on the trial of Adolph Eichmann.[1] The term *banal* means "obvious" and "boring," something that is unremarkable. One of the principal architects of the Holocaust, the balding, bespectacled Eichmann looked more like an everyday bank clerk than an executioner responsible for genocide. He claimed to have no particular hatred for Jews. In fact, he insisted he had been just obeying orders as he helped design the Final Solution to murder millions of innocent men, women, and children.

Often evil looks more like Eichmann than a madman screaming hatred. Evil can wear a nurse's coat, a lawyer's suit, or a minister's robe. Evil can come softly. Just as Lucifer himself can masquerade as an angel of light (2 Corinthians 11:14), the greatest injustices can be presented as justice, and the greatest lies as truth.

Evil can also stand as a ruling of "justice," handed down by the highest court of one of the freest countries in the world. In the 1973 *Roe v. Wade* decision, seven US Supreme Court Justices—all men—ruled that abortion was a constitutional right for women. Their ruling would dramatically alter American life. In the decades that followed, while abortion was presented as the wise or even compassionate solution to problems, it is estimated that more than sixty million children were killed in utero.[2]

Decades earlier, a seemingly ordinary middle-class American activist named Margaret Sanger founded an institution that would lead the industry responsible for killing more innocent people than any twentieth-century genocidal regime. Sanger's creation, what would become the billion-dollar corporation known today as Planned Parenthood, now commits nearly half the nation's abortions. Currently, that means they are responsible for killing nearly a thousand children in America every day.[3]

A proud eugenicist and a matter-of-fact dehumanizer, Sanger viewed herself and her allies as champions of progress and women's rights. She would not have been a champion of a family like mine. "The most merciful thing that the large family does to one of its infant members," Sanger said unashamedly, "is to kill it."[4] Taking its cue from its founder, Planned Parenthood would go on to kill millions of American children and advocate against every single proposed abortion restriction.

Yet many Americans today rarely think about abortion or consider it evil. Similarly, during Hitler's regime, most Germans failed to see the evil around them, much less stand against it. The few who did recognize the evil of the Nazis and spoke out against them were brutally silenced. Appalled by her government's treatment of Jews, twenty-one-year-old student Sophie Scholl resisted by distributing anti-Nazi literature at the University of Munich. For this simple act of defiance, Sophie was arrested and promptly beheaded. Other would-be resisters got the message: speaking the truth about evil comes at a great cost. Exposing darkness is still a high-risk endeavor in any country, even in the United States where freedom of speech is both prized and protected by the First Amendment.

It's one thing to look back on history and imagine that the genocides of the twentieth century were unique to those who committed them, or that we might have seen things differently had we lived in that time and place. However, it is folly to think we are somehow wiser than past generations. We share the same wounded human nature as our ancestors. To avoid making the same errors as generations past, we must study those errors and learn from them. We need to pay attention to what is happening around us and be alert to the evils we may have become blind to. God willing, future generations may view abortion in much the same way as we view slavery and the Holocaust.

In my teens I cared about many causes—from ending homelessness and helping earthquake victims overseas to caring for those with disabilities. But I could not forget the images I had seen of children killed by abortion any more than I could forget the ultrasound image of Caterina inside my mother's womb. The contrast between the images was stark. It weighed on me, and I tried to think of ways I could make a difference. As I came to see, abortion has taken more human lives than any other injustice in our history. I sensed, too, that our spiritual survival as a civilization hinged on whether we allowed the bloodshed to continue. A series of events, starting with the book I read when I was nine, convinced me that my cause should be life itself.

I was eleven when a friend and I decided to write a public letter to the adults in our community asking them to vote for life in the next election. I typed it up on my parents' desktop computer and printed out a few dozen copies, which took almost an hour because our printer was so slow. "We are only eleven and fourteen, and not old enough to vote for life. But you are," the letter began.

We taped the letter to the walls outside our local supermarket and pharmacy. It felt like a shot in the dark, and it was a one-time deal. Elections only happened every few years, and I estimated that maybe a few hundred people would even see it. What else could I do? I wanted to join a pro-life group and get more involved, but despite asking around and researching online, I could not find one in San Jose. I was busy with school and extracurricular activities, and time went by.

Two years later, I discovered through the community pregnancy center that there was a small group of people who met outside an abortion facility in San Jose every Saturday to pray and offer resources to women entering the facility. I learned that through their faithful presence out-side the clinic and their sincere offers of help, they were able to persuade dozens of women to cancel their abortion appointments and choose life for their babies.

After negotiating with my parents for permission, I arranged with a couple of friends to go to the clinic one Saturday. One of my friends, Dev, had his driver's license and got permission to drive me and another friend to the clinic. I had printed out materials about the local pregnancy center to hand to any woman willing to take them. We all made small talk as we drove, nervous about what the day might be like.

We parked a few blocks away. As we walked to the clinic, I mar-veled at how ordinary the neighborhood seemed. A children's daycare was across the street next to a YMCA. Cars drove by, and families dropped off their little ones right across from Planned Parenthood's abortion clinic, one of several abortion centers in San Jose.

This multistory brick building towered over the street. Its reflective windows prevented curious eyes from looking in, and a fence kept pro-testors at bay. Little did I know at the time how large Planned Parenthood would loom in my life. At the time, though, I marveled that this building had been standing there throughout my entire childhood, just fifteen miles away from my house, and I had not known about it.

This clinic killed preborn children between the ages of seven weeks and twenty-four weeks. At only three and a half weeks, a child's heart has begun to beat. By seven weeks, their arms and legs are already beginning to form. Some babies could survive at just twenty-two weeks with medical support. Entering into that clinic, every child within a mother's womb had a beating heart and a future. Each was as precious and as holy as any other human on earth.

At the front of the clinic, we met up with Gary, a tall, gray-bearded man in his forties with a kind face. I would learn later that before Gary's conversion, he and his girlfriend got pregnant and had a child together. When she got pregnant a second time, Gary told her, "It's your problem;

you take care of it." She had the abortion. Years later, Gary went to a pro-life talk that shared our need to be saved from our sin by Christ. Deeply grieved that he had encouraged the killing of his own child, Gary asked God for forgiveness. The love and forgiveness of Christ radically changed Gary's life. Filled with hope that he could help others after Christ had transformed his own life, Gary would spend decades praying and offering resources and care to women outside abortion clinics.

I had gotten in touch with Gary through my friend Francesca from the pregnancy center. Although I had spoken with Gary on the phone, I had never met him. Francesca told me Gary was there every Saturday and was sometimes joined by friends or elderly ladies from a local Catholic church who prayed the rosary. Standing outside the clinic, Gary greeted us warmly.

"I'm so glad you three are here!" he said happily, then added quietly, "It's a busy day today."

We watched as cars drove into the parking lot next to the building and parked. A young girl exited the passenger door of a white Suburban. The driver, who looked as if she could have been the girl's mother, stepped out beside her. The girl's face was crumpled, her eyes filled with tears. Her mother looked stoic. Gary called out over the short fence, "You don't have to do this! There are people who want to help you!"

A heavy-set, bearded man with gray hair, wearing a bright orange vest that read ESCORT walked quickly over to the women. "Don't listen to what he's saying," the escort said loudly. "Just walk this way." As he hurried the women across the lot to the back door of the building, Gary's voice called after them, "We're here to help you. We love you and your baby!"

The girl and her mother disappeared into the building. Car after car drove into the parking lot. The women were driven by boyfriends, husbands, mothers, sisters, friends. Some drivers dropped off the women and kept going. Other drivers remained in their cars. Still others accompanied the pregnant young women into the clinic. As each person approached the building, Gary called out, offering help and resources.

My friends and I stood next to Gary on the sidewalk, praying quietly. I knew that a dozen yards or so away from me, behind the brick and steel, was an operating room. Each of these women entered that room nurturing a baby within. The abortionist would enter soon after and would tear that baby, that precious life, into pieces. He did it legally. There was no one to stop it. It was a "woman's right," even if the woman was just a young girl who may or may not have been coerced into being there.

After some time, the number of cars slowed and no more young women came. Quietly, my friends and I walked back to the car. I didn't know what to say or do at that moment. I had seen death and hopelessness play out right in front of me, and I had little power to prevent any of it. The world did not seem to care.

We were quiet as we started the drive home. After a few minutes, Dev said, "Want to stop at In-N-Out?" I looked at him, unsure of what to say. How could we go and eat hamburgers after watching dozens of women enter a building where their preborn children would die? How could we go about doing anything normal? It wasn't that my friend didn't care. Going to get lunch was a perfectly normal thing to do. But after being so close to so much pain, despair, and death, I knew I'd never be the same. I may not have accomplished much that day on the sidewalk, but the experience changed me.

I began to think seriously about devoting my life to pro-life work. Unlike other abuses such as sex trafficking or child abuse, abortion was legal. In a nation that claimed to defend basic human rights, beginning with the right to life, these children were being killed with the explicit permission of the law and at the request of their own mothers. These children had no way to defend themselves. In the womb, they were totally dependent on their mothers, unable to even cry out for help. Among the victims of all the injustices throughout the world, babies are the most powerless. And there was no ignoring the staggering death toll.

At the time, more than one million children were being killed every year in the United States alone.[5] Worldwide, the number was closer to fifty million each year.[6] The sheer number of lives lost daily eclipsed any other single cause of death for human beings. The reality was undeniable: the world was turning a blind eye to the legal murder of more than one hundred thousand defenseless children every day. It's been said that "a single death is a tragedy; a million deaths is a statistic." As horrifying as that statement is, it also makes a point—it is possible to become numb to evil in high numbers. Coming to grips with this, I came to see abortion as the greatest human rights abuse of our time.

The first right of every human being is the right to life. The US Declaration of Independence states that every human being is endowed with "certain unalienable rights, that among these are life, liberty, and the pursuit of happiness." The right to life comes first, preceding the rights to liberty and the pursuit of happiness. If we do not protect that first right, no other rights matter. Other injustices can be righted. Other abuses can be stopped. Other wounds can be healed. For the child who endures abortion, there is no righting, no stopping, no healing. A baby is either dead or alive. Once he or she is killed, there is no way to restore a baby's rights. An abortion cannot be undone.

As I grew in my devotion to Christ, my faith also guided me to focus on the pro-life cause. Beyond the prohibition against murder, the Bible is full of verses that acknowledge the humanity and sacredness of a child in the womb. In the Psalms, King David praised God for the mystery of creation: "For you formed my inward parts; you knitted me together in my mother's womb. I praise you, for I am fearfully and wonderfully made. Wonderful are your works" (139:13–14 ESV). The Didache, a catechism for early Christians in the first three centuries of the church, explicitly prohibits abortion.

The Bible also provides strong exhortations for our responsibility to help those in need. James reminds us, "Religion that is pure and undefiled before God, the Father, is this: to care for orphans and widows in their distress" (James 1:27 NRSVCE). What child is more orphaned than the one who is in danger of abortion? I also was struck by Jesus' statement, "Truly

I tell you, just as you did not do it to one of the least of these, you did not do it to me" (Matthew 25:45 NRSVCE). A child in the womb, in danger of abortion, is certainly among the "least of these."

There are many causes that need our attention and that are worthy of our concern, but the greatest need in our era is ultimately spiritual. "Jesus is thirsting for our love," said Mother Teresa, "and this is the thirst of everyone, poor and rich alike."[7] Before fully committing to a cause, I had to ask myself—as we all should—Where is the need the greatest? Who most needs the advocacy but has the least support? Where is the suffering the most profound, both physically and spiritually? And what immediate difference could I make?

In choosing a cause, we have to be wary of those causes that may appear attractive but which can be ultimately destructive. A cause can be well intentioned but become destructive when it is based on an incomplete or incorrect understanding of the human person.

Take, for example, the cause of Marxism. In high school, my friend Jacob decided he was a Marxist after reading *The Communist Manifesto*. Communism was Karl Marx's great cause. Jacob and I had long talks about it. He even sewed onto his favorite burgundy sweatshirt a Soviet Communist insignia, the hammer and sickle, which represented sympathy with the proletariat or "working men." We'd walk around the community college campus where we took some of our high school classes, like two young revolutionaries, dreaming about a utopian future.

We weren't that unique in our exploration of Marxism. Many young people are attracted to the idealistic promises of communism and socialism. When I first read *The Communist Manifesto*, I found parts of it inspiring. The ideal—that we are all brothers and sisters responsible for one another—was appealing. So was the idea that the worker had dignity. Although Marx did not live long enough to see what would happen to his ideal, Jacob and I had no excuse for our ignorance except for our youth. As I learned over time, communism almost inevitably produces leaders such as Lenin and Stalin and Mao and results in forced labor camps, political assassinations, religious oppression, elimination of free speech, confiscation of private property, and the murder of millions of innocent people. If there was ever a destructive cause, this was one.

Karl Marx had attempted to build his utopia on a faulty foundation. He thought that human beings, not God, were the ultimate source of morality. In fact, for Marx, there was no God. He viewed human beings not as free individuals with inherent dignity, but as cogs in a class system who were constantly at war with one another. In other words, Marx was a materialist, reducing the human person to matter and failing to recognize their moral agency. Marx's fatal mistake was to misunderstand both human nature and God.

Another false cause that has led to great evil over the last century is eugenics, the belief that we can improve the human condition by controlling who gets to have children. This movement rejects the dignity of human beings, viewing the sick, the poor, those deemed "racially inferior," and the disabled as unfit members of the population whose very existence should be prevented. In the United States, this movement reached its peak of acceptability in 1927. In the now infamous case *Buck v. Bell*, the US Supreme Court decreed that Carrie Buck, a white woman from Virginia, was mentally defective and thus could be forcefully sterilized. By court decree and against her will, doctors forcibly operated on her, tying her fallopian tubes so she would not be able to bear children.

"It is better for all the world," wrote famed liberal Supreme Court Justice Oliver Wendell Holmes, Jr., "if instead of waiting to execute degenerate offspring for crime, or to let them starve for their imbecility, society can prevent those who are manifestly unfit from continuing their kind."[8] Today, many use similar reasoning to argue for abortion: it's better for a poor or disadvantaged woman to choose abortion so that her child won't grow up poor or disadvantaged.

Planned Parenthood founder Margaret Sanger approved wholeheartedly of this philosophy. Her goal, after all, was to "grasp Utopia from the skies and plant it on earth."[9] In her rejection of God, however, Sanger was forever improvising what form her utopia should take. Whatever form it took, her utopia would have no place for the "mentally defective,"[10] which, in her writings, included the poor, the disabled, essentially all African Americans, and most other people of color. She argued that preventing "defectives" from being born was the height of compassion. Eugenics remained hugely popular in the Western world until Adolph Hitler put its principles into action and people saw only too clearly where those principles led.

Sadly, many people today still hold eugenic ideals without even realizing it. For example, children with disabilities are routinely killed before birth because they are deemed unfit. Using the same justification as many eugenicists of the past, proponents of aborting babies with prenatal diagnoses argue that it is more compassionate to kill them than to let them live with their disability or to die naturally of a life-threatening condition. Parents are often encouraged to get prenatal screenings of their children so they can abort a child who has a genetic disorder or physical defects. In the United States, this has resulted in the selective abortion of an estimated 40 percent of all preborn Down syndrome babies.[11] In Iceland, that figure approaches 100 percent.

I understand the pressure, especially on my generation, by some powerful institutions to join false causes. Many major corporations, media groups, tech companies, and much of our education establishments promote the legalized killing of children in the womb as a crucial "cause" for women. It's why doing our homework is just as important as opening our hearts.

My cause was to fight for life. Abortion was an injustice I could do something about. I could educate my peers. I could raise money for pregnancy resource centers. I could be a silent witness outside abortion facilities. Nothing held me back from helping at least one young woman who struggled with an abortion decision. Nothing held me back from trying to save at least one life. How many other causes allow an ordinary individual to directly help save a life?

If you know what breaks your heart, if you discover who your heroes are, if you are confident in what you believe, and if you have examined the facts to avoid going down a misguided path, you will be well positioned to find your cause. Remember: your existence at this particular time in human history is no accident. The gifts and talents you have are not random. Although the work we do and the talents we have may not initially appear to be a perfect match to the myriad needs and problems of the world, applying our gifts in service to others is part of what we have been made for. Aligning our talents to address the needs around us is a struggle that refines and strengthens us. It helps us grow into the men and women God created us to be. To refuse to struggle, to refuse to try, is to refuse to grow.

When we open our eyes to the greatest evils of our day, we become alert to the suffering and injustice they inflict. There we will find many causes waiting to be championed by those willing to fight.

CHAPTER 7

Just Start

I knew I had to do more. It wasn't enough to stand outside an abortion clinic with a few friends, helplessly watching women and girls walk into that death center. I had read books, scoured websites, and researched how Planned Parenthood and their allies defended the killing. But what good was my knowledge if I didn't share it? I thought that if we could educate our peers about the horror of abortion as well as about the goodness of life and the many people and resources available to help mothers and children in need, we could prevent women and girls from ever going in.

But there was a challenge—I still couldn't find a pro-life group to join. In the entire San Francisco Bay Area, there were apparently no pro-life groups that focused on youth education. How could there be no pro-life youth presence in a region with millions of people? The closest I came to finding something was the Peers Encouraging Abstinence Team, a group led by our local community pregnancy center. I had to start somewhere, so I started there. They were a group of high school freshmen and sopho-mores who gave presentations to junior high students, encouraging them to avoid sexual activity before marriage. Thinking that less sexual activity among teens could only help decrease the abortion rate, I decided to join.

As part of our presentations, we each had a persona to act out in various skits. I was the token virgin on the team, there to serve as an example that, yes, it was possible and acceptable to be a virgin in high school. Abortion wasn't discussed, but we discussed STIs, teen pregnancy, and, of course, the morality of sex and the psychological and emotional pain that often comes with early sexual experience.

Seeing the impact of those skits gave me an idea. Could we give presentations on abortion and sex to more students? Not knowing where to find guidance, I went to the Internet and continued researching. I also started cold-calling California pro-life organizations and national youth organizations. Along the way, I began praying, "Use me, God. Use me to help save lives."

Eventually, a friend from my school debate club who knew about my search for a pro-life group gave me the phone number for nineteen-year-old Jonathan Keller, a friend of her family. He lived in Fresno, several hours away, and worked for a group called Fresno Right to Life. I found the group's website, which described how the group presented educational programs to youth. This sounded exactly like what I hoped to do. Not exactly sure of what to say, I dialed his number.

"Hello, this is Jonathan Keller."

I kept it simple. "Hi, my name is Lila. I'm fourteen. I want to start a pro-life club. I have some friends who are interested too. Can you help me?"

The voice on the other end of the phone was friendly but uncertain and a little surprised. "Uh, sure. Hi, Lila, nice to meet you. That's great. We do a lot of youth events in Fresno—"

"I'm in San Jose," I interrupted. I already knew they were in Fresno, which was more than three hours away. Since I had no license, much less a car, I put it to him straight: "Would you be able to come up here?"

There was a moment of silence on the other end of the line.

"Um, we only do work in Fresno. But let me talk to my boss."

Thankfully, Jonathan was able to venture beyond his usual job description in Fresno and head to the Bay Area. Always generous and up for a challenge, he was happy to help our little group of aspiring pro-life activists. It was a good thing my parents' house had such an open-door policy too. Friends and relatives routinely came and went, often spending the night on the couch downstairs. My parents said Jonathan was welcome to stay over a weekend to train us. Looking back, I see how these acts of generosity by my hardworking parents made possible so much of my earliest activism.

I got together a group of several friends and our pro-life club was born. For two days, seated on couches in my parents' living room, we learned pro-life apologetics and presentation skills on topics such as fetal development and abortion risks. For faith audiences, we learned biblical truths we could apply to abortion. Jonathan would return to San Jose several more times to continue training us, and over the next several months, we all became proficient in pro-life apologetics. This time of intense studying and training was key and would lay the foundation for much of my future work.

Our goal was to give a presentation to every student in the San Francisco Bay Area. Even at fourteen, however, I understood that schools and youth groups would not exactly be eager to welcome a group of teenagers wanting to talk to them about something as controversial as abortion. To close our first sale, we needed to find someone willing to let us present.

I thought my best bet might be our family's faith community. I grew up going to a Bible church in Saratoga, a beautiful area just west of San Jose in which home prices had risen exponentially as Silicon Valley emerged as the hub for the world's booming tech industry. The church reflected its now well-heeled neighborhood.

Like many churches, abortion was almost never talked about at our church even though, at the time, more than one million women were having an abortion each year. The abortion industry's own surveys show that 70 percent of American women who had abortions considered themselves Protestant or Catholic, and one in five of those who had an abortion were adolescent girls.[1]

Despite the prevalence of abortion, even among churchgoers, our pastors never addressed the topic at youth group and would very rarely address it with the larger congregation. Statistically, however, it was inevitable that many women—and men—at my church had been affected by abortion. I decided to call one of my pastors and point-blank ask for permission to give a presentation. One of our youth leaders, whom I'll call Scott, was a fun-loving, kind, and gregarious man. The conversation went something like this:

"Hey, is this Pastor Scott?"

"This is he! Who is this?"

"This is Lila Rose. I'm from your youth group."

"Of course! Hey, Lila! So great to hear from you. What's going on?"

"Well, I had something I wanted to talk to you about. I wanted to get your advice on something. Can I meet with you next Sunday?"

I lost the nerve to ask over the phone, and that was probably for the best. Phone asks are rarely as effective as in-person asks. Even so, it took a full year of work to finally convince our pastors to allow our pro-life group to come and talk about abortion. My friends and I had to meet with our pastors multiple times to explain exactly what we planned to do, show each the presentation in detail, make some compromises on the material, and more. But in the end, we got our shot. Three friends and I stood before my youth group of about forty kids on a Sunday morning and presented a PowerPoint and videos educating them about abortion.

We showed images of embryonic and fetal development. At the moment of fertilization, when the egg is fertilized by sperm, a unique, individual human being comes into existence. We explained that we all began our lives as a single-cell embryo, and even then, we were alive and growing. As a tiny embryo, all our genetic material is present, with eye color, height, skin tone, and a million other characteristics already predetermined.

We shared pro-life author Scott Klusendorf's analysis that for all nine months in the womb, the only differences between the child growing within and any born human being are Size, Level of Development, Environment, and Degree of Dependency—SLED, for short. The differences in size between a fetus and a toddler, the differences in body development, the different environments they live in, and the degree to which we are all dependent on other people (and uniquely dependent on our mothers at the beginning of our lives) to survive at different stages of our lives—none of these justify the lethal discrimination of abortion.[2]

We also discussed the "hard cases" of abortion—the tiny percentage of cases due to rape, incest, or risk to the life of the mother. The rape of a woman is a terrible crime, and caring for a child unexpectedly is difficult, but the forced extraction and killing of a child is also a terrible crime and trauma to carry for the rest of the woman's life. The child is totally innocent and does not deserve to die because of the crimes of his or her father. An abortion cannot take away the trauma of a rape; it can only add the trauma of an abortion. And while some serious medical conditions may rarely require the early delivery of the child, this is not an abortion.

Abortion is a violent and destructive, forced and premature removal of the child from the pregnant woman, with the intention of killing the child. Early abortions, in the first trimester, typically use suction instruments to rip the developing baby apart and out of the womb. Increasingly over the past twenty years, the drug Mifepristone or RU486 has been pushed by the abortion industry to poison and kill the developing child and then deliver in an artificial miscarriage. Later abortions in the second trimester are typically done using forceps to rip the baby out of the womb, whole or in pieces. At later stages and in the third trimester, abortionists may kill the preborn child with a chemical injection first, before tearing him or her apart with forceps or inducing labor of the stillborn baby.

The feedback after our talk was overwhelmingly positive. "I'm definitely pro-life now," shared one girl.

With one successful presentation behind us, I realized that a more professional sounding name than "pro-life club" would probably help us secure more speaking events. During a club meeting in my family's living room one evening, our group tossed around names. I wanted something with the word *action* in it and a little mystery. Taking action would be critical to our mission. Finally, I said, "How about 'Live Action'?" One friend joked, "That's a dumb idea." I laughed and declared, "That's the name!"

Within a year, we were giving presentations across the Bay Area. Eventually I would meet my friend Ignacio after giving a presentation with his older sister, Francesca. Courageous and determined, Ignacio would help Live Action San Jose grow dramatically. Fluent in Spanish, he would also found our bilingual presentation program. He became a core part of my team, and together we reached thousands of teens and young adults throughout the Bay Area.

When I launched Live Action, it never occurred to me that I might fail. I didn't waste time doubting whether we could make a difference. I focused my energy on finding something I could do, even if it was as simple as picking up the phone and cold-calling for help. In the beginning, most of my time was invested in learning everything I could about my cause. After a lot of trial and error, I found simple ways to get started. At the time, I could not have imagined what Live Action would later become. I simply knew I wanted to educate my peers and maybe save one life that way, and so I was determined to try.

Ask yourself: What is one thing you can do today? Maybe it's learning more about your cause by reading a book or listening to a talk or making a plan to show up at an event. Maybe it's calling someone you know is more experienced and asking questions. Maybe it's researching other groups already in the fight. Often the greatest efforts begin quietly, with a simple action. You don't need a master strategy to start fighting for your cause. You don't need years of experience. You need a willingness to study and learn and to enter the battle even when the path is unclear. You have everything you need right now to begin.

The trick is just to start.

PART 2

OVERCOMING

CHAPTER 8

Prepare to Stand Alone

My high school pro-life club met Wednesday nights. On one particular Wednesday morning, I called or texted all the club members to remind them about our meeting as I always did: "Hey! Just calling to remind you about tonight. We're gonna be running through our presentation for our event in three weeks."

This time everyone had an excuse. "Oh, I'm sorry, Li. I'm behind on homework and can't make it." "I have other plans." "My mom wants to do a family movie night." "I just can't make it."

No one was coming. Frustrated and disappointed, I couldn't understand why my friends didn't prioritize our pro-life work. Couldn't they see that lives were on the line?

"The meeting tonight is canceled," I told my mom.

"Oh no, what happened?"

"Everyone is too busy to come," I said. She could see the disappointment in my face.

"I'm sorry to hear that."

"It's just frustrating when no one else seems to take this very seriously." I sighed. "What am I doing wrong?"

My mom looked at me sympathetically and said, "Leadership is lonely, Lila. Sometimes we have to go it alone. But if we keep going and never give up, eventually, people will follow."

Ten years later, millions would be following Live Action, the pro-life educational nonprofit I would go on to build. They followed because they, too, believed in the cause to protect innocent human life. But that following didn't happen overnight, or in a month, or even in a year. And I had to start even when I didn't know what I was doing and even when I was alone.

Sometimes the toughest battles are the ones nobody else sees, the ones in our minds. When beginning our mission, the first obstacles we may face are our own fears and doubts. If our minds are sabotaging our efforts, we will always struggle to make progress.

What are the fears? We may worry about what other people think of us. We may wonder, *Will people disapprove of me? Will they think my cause is wrong? Will they reject me?*

What are the doubts? We may wonder whether we have what it takes to actually make a difference. We may ask ourselves, *What difference can I possibly make? I don't know what to do. I'm not sure what to say.*

Working for any cause is challenging, but there is a unique challenge when taking up a cause perceived as countercultural or controversial. Safe causes can be easier. No one discouraged my high school best friend and me from raising money for famine victims in Niger. No one was offended when, as a fifteen-year-old, I went to Tijuana, Mexico, with our church group to help build houses for the poor. No one objected when I went to Morocco at eighteen to help earthquake victims. And the Sunday school teachers at my parents' church praised me when I volunteered to care for a child with disabilities during the services.

These were all worthy causes. Helping people in need is always important. These efforts require determination, grit, and creativity. A new test for all of us, however, may come when we take on a cause not everyone agrees with. These are the unsafe causes—the causes that can be derailed by self-consciousness and questions about what people might think of us.

Media can have a significant influence over what is considered a safe or unsafe cause. For example, when I was a high school student, a local San Jose newspaper did a feature story celebrating our fundraising campaign for famine victims in Niger. The reporter met my friend and me at a local bagel shop and congratulated us on our humanitarian efforts. Famine relief is a safe cause. Years later, the San Jose media also took notice of my pro-life work. But the feature piece they wrote about Live Action was critical and condescending. Abortion is an unsafe cause. In the media's eyes, Live Action was controversial and not in a good way.

This is not to suggest that a controversial cause is more important than an uncontroversial cause, but it is to say we should not shy away from causes simply because they may be controversial. In the nineteenth century, for instance, to stand against slavery was highly controversial. It often meant standing alone. Abolitionists risked public scorn, the loss of their livelihoods, and violence, but had the controversy discouraged them from standing up for justice, the evil of slavery would have gone unchallenged. Even into the twentieth century, it took great courage for women to stand up for the right to vote. The women who went public with their protest endured ridicule—from both men and women.

But those abolitionists and suffragettes were not primarily concerned with what others thought of them: they were confident in their causes. I think that is key for us. If we are confident in our causes, if we understand the why behind what we are fighting for, we will be less concerned with the opinions of others. We will not worry so much about being understood or being accepted. And our confidence will win others over.

What about the fear that we may not be qualified to fight for our cause? Over the years, there have been many times when my own self-doubts have bred in me a complex called the imposter syndrome. While imposter syndrome is not an official diagnosis, many psychologists acknowledge that high-achievers are often plagued with chronic self-doubt. Imposter syndrome sufferers often feel they have no right to be doing the work they are doing. They think they lack the credentials or the talent or the character and often feel afraid someone will figure it out.

I've experienced bouts of imposter syndrome over the years. The reality is, I *was* in over my head from the beginning. As I've shared, I started Live Action when I was fifteen. I started doing investigative reporting as an eighteen-year-old freshman at UCLA, the biggest university in California and, in many ways, one hostile to my cause. I had little formal training in journalism. My school didn't even offer a journalism major, but I saw a tremendous need, and I felt strongly that I had to try to fill it.

My first undercover investigation of Los Angeles abortion facilities exposed their willingness to cover up child sexual abuse. As a result of that investigation, I did my first television interview while still a freshman, not on a local show with a limited audience, but on a number-one-rated national cable news show. There wasn't much time for practice. I was thrown into the deep end of the pool from the beginning. Certain friends fell out of my life, and acquaintances railed against me on social media. It hurt, but what would have hurt more was inaction, because lives were on the line. That's when I realized that I could choose some of my hurts, just as I could choose to push through my doubts.

And there were many opportunities for doubt. I was just nineteen when Live Action earned nonprofit status. I gave my first briefing to members of Congress at twenty-one while I was still in college. I raised my first million dollars at twenty-two. I hosted my first congressional press conference, with dozens of Congress people and media groups, at twenty-three (and I made a very embarrassing mistake—more about that in another chapter). I say this not to brag, but to confess—I was learning every uncertain step of the way.

While I had personal heroes and mentors, no one had gone before me and charted a similar route and then told me exactly how to follow. There was no detailed instruction manual. And although I had help—generous and wise souls who accompanied me at various moments in the journey—I had no cofounder.

The path wasn't marked out for me. It still isn't. And it's unlikely to be for you, or for any of us trying to forge a new path of change.

You may feel like an imposter when you begin your mission, but you aren't. You're a brave soul who is willing to stand up even when others won't and give the best of what you have. Don't buy into the creeping doubts telling you that you can't stand up, that you shouldn't speak, that you won't make a difference. Your cause is waiting. You can do this.

My best advice for you as you begin your fight even in the midst of doubt is this: Lean in to your conviction. Let your passion drive you. For me, knowing I was fighting to help save the life of even one child overrode my own feelings of inadequacy and insecurity. If we are focused enough on what and for whom we are fighting, our desire to make a difference will overcome our fear of failure. We discover true courage when we feel our fears and admit our doubts and then try anyway.

The reality is, we are all imposters when we first begin. Qualification comes with practice. And there is no more effective practice than on-the-job experience. Practice isn't faking it. It's learning. To learn, we have to be ready to make mistakes, and we have to be willing to get back up even after an embarrassing fall. If we constantly give in to self-doubt or worry that the world will think less of us, we can talk ourselves out of fighting for the best of causes before we've even begun.

We cannot afford to leave the great work of our world's most pressing causes to others because we imagine they are somehow more prepared, better qualified, or simply braver. Instead, we can look to those who have gone before us, learn what we can, and courageously get to work. We need to cultivate that little fire in our souls, that desire to stand up and fight for what is right—and do so carefully. Self-doubt is a swift extinguisher, so ignore it. We can develop our abilities through our experiences and through formal study under able teachers. To nurture those abilities, we have to seek out the heroes, mentors, and coaches who can teach us and help us (more on mentors and coaches in chapters 14 and 15).

Saint Joan of Arc, one of my heroes and my confirmation saint, famously said, "Act, and God will act."[1] Confident in her calling, this teenage French girl set out alone to do the unthinkable and the seemingly impossible, leading thousands of soldiers to historic victories against English occupation. Ultimately, it was her faith in God that gave her the courage. Later, even in the face of rejection, betrayal, and execution, she chose to trust. It was God, not the world, who had both called and qualified her. Her dogged faith in an all-powerful, all-loving God empowered her to fight for what was right, no matter the cost.

When beginning any endeavor, I have found it rare that everyone in my life supported or understood what I was trying to do, and rarer still that I felt fully confident I would succeed. During my years of activism, I lost friends because they disapproved of what I was doing. However, I also discovered over time that there were many others out there who believed as I did but either were too nervous to take a stand or did not know where to start. I believe the same will be true for you. Your willingness to stand alone will set an example for those around you. Your courage will inspire others.

CHAPTER 9

Leave Your Comfort Zone

During my junior year of high school, I spent hours poring over catalogues trying to decide which colleges to apply to. Beyond getting a degree, I felt that going to college would give me the opportunity to reach more students with the pro-life message and possibly to save more lives. I considered some liberal arts schools, such as the University of Chicago, and I even won a scholarship to Hillsdale, a top conservative liberal arts college in Michigan.

Hillsdale had been my dream college throughout high school. I loved the idea of studying the great literature of Western civilization with like-minded, passionate peers. But I decided that while I needed to continue studying, I didn't want to attend a school where most of the students already knew that abortion was wrong. Instead, I wanted to go where there was a lot of need, where students might never hear the pro-life message. I debated between UC Berkeley and UCLA and ultimately landed on UCLA. It was bigger than Berkeley, and it was located in the heart of the world's entertainment capital. I decided there would be more opportunity to spread the pro-life message there. UCLA was where my mission took me next.

Wherever I went, I knew there would be women at risk and lives in danger. Planned Parenthood, the nation's largest abortion chain, had been targeting college-aged women for years. Knowing that women between the ages of eighteen and twenty-four have 44 percent of all abortions,[1] Planned Parenthood is strategic in targeting them. For example, the Planned Parenthood Generation Action Network is "a network of young organizers and activists across the country who organize events on their campuses and in their communities to mobilize advocates for reproductive freedom."[2] I didn't know exactly how I would fight back against Planned Parenthood once on campus, but I would do my best to figure it out.

I also understood how young pregnant women, especially college students, could feel pressure to get an abortion. By the time they got to college, students understood the stigma and stress of being pregnant, were wary of the adoption process, and were afraid of how an unwanted baby would interfere with the plans they had for their lives. These students would be especially susceptible to abortion propaganda.

Unmarried and feeling financially and emotionally unprepared for a baby, many young women listen when told that abortion is the right choice. Some women have chosen abortion for no deeper reason than to maintain their lifestyle. Abortion advocates never admit this, but if data from the state of Florida is any indication, at least 75 percent of abortions in this country could be "elective," meaning they are likely committed for the convenience of the mother. And that number doesn't include abortions done for social, economic, or emotional concerns.[3]

UCLA, forty thousand students strong, offered me a lot of opportunity to do some good. With such a large student body, I also thought I would find many other pro-life students with whom I could team up. Packing my suitcase and leaving my parents' home for Los Angeles, I felt the nervous anticipation that most first-year college-bound students feel, but wrapped up in the anticipation was also a strong sense of calling. I felt I was on a pro-life mission, not just an educational mission.

During my first week at UCLA, I applied the same strategy I had used in my high school years: Find out who was already doing pro-life work and join them. If such an organization didn't exist, I'd start one. After attending the UCLA freshman activity fair, starting one seemed like the only option. Among hundreds of tables set up in a long line of tents, I could not find a single table representing a pro-life club.

Surely, among the forty thousand students, there had to be other pro-lifers. It turned out I was right. A few days later, I noticed a table on Bruin Walk with a sign that read, "Are You Pro-Life?" Sitting at the table reading a book was a tall girl in a wide-brimmed straw hat.

"Hey! Thank you for being here!" I greeted her. "My name is Lila, and I'm pro-life too!"

She looked up from her book. "That's great! Nice to meet you. I'm Esther."

Not wanting to be late for class, I set up a meeting to connect with her later. Esther was the vice president of Bruins for Life, and she would be joined by her president, Liz. The next day, we met outside and sat at a picnic table. Esther and Liz were both seniors who would graduate at the end of that school year.

"It's so great you're a freshman," said Liz cheerfully, taking charge of our meeting. "Otherwise the club might die out."

"Die out?" I asked, alarmed. "Aren't there other people in the group?"

"You're looking at the group," Liz said.

"It's just the two of you?" I was shocked that a campus of forty thousand would have only two students willing to stand up for life. Were there really only three of us?

I would find out later that there had been several others in the club, but they had almost all graduated the previous year, leaving Liz and Esther as the only leaders. They were on the hunt for new recruits, and freshmen like me would have the longest shelf life.

"Would you like to be the club treasurer?" Liz offered.

"Well, sure," I answered tentatively. "How much money do you have in the bank?"

"Well, we don't have a bank account," said Esther. "But we could get one."

"Where do you keep your money?"

They explained they didn't have any, but that we could raise money and use it to host events. I felt a growing anxiety as we talked. There was so much to do! And I felt there had to be other pro-life students on campus. We just had to find them and rally them.

"I really appreciate that you are both involved in pro-life," I said, "but I think I need to start another group. I came to UCLA to do pro-life activism." I told them about what we'd been doing in San Jose. "I'd like to bring the strategies I've learned there to this campus."

"That's great," said Liz enthusiastically. "But you don't need to start another group! How about you just be president?"

I was impressed by how humble and eager she was to hand me her position. Both Esther and Liz graciously accepted the name change from Bruins for Life to Live Action UCLA, and we started planning events. I found out later that they had been praying specifically for a new freshman to help grow the pro-life club at UCLA. Liz, who would become a dear lifelong friend, came from a strong family tradition of pro-life advocacy. Her dad, Dr. T. Murphy Goodwin, was a leading perinatologist and a well-known pro-life advocate. Later on, Esther introduced me to a women's center near campus that would change my life (more on that in chapter 12). As we three joined forces, our little group would go on to recruit dozens of students in the coming months.

During my freshman orientation, administrators performed a skit about condom use and the importance of "safe sex." They joked that while there might be virgins in the audience, it was unlikely we'd stay that way for long. The freshman class was told the virtues of "practicing protection," and the healthcare center on campus had bowls of condoms on its counters.

I found it sad and offensive that UCLA thought so little of their students that while it expected the best of us academically, it expected the least of us when it came to sexual morality. UCLA administrators clearly expected students to have sex and therefore encouraged the use of contraceptives. The reality, however, is that even when used regularly, contraceptives are far from 100 percent effective. For example, according to the Centers for Disease Control, condoms have a 13 percent failure rate, diaphragms a 17 percent failure rate, and spermicides a 21 percent failure rate. In fact, according to Planned Parenthood's research arm, the Guttmacher Institute, half of the women who sought an abortion were using a contraceptive in the month they got pregnant.[4] On a campus where sex was encouraged and drinking and drugs were common, contraception use could be hit or miss. What then?

I wondered how many students at UCLA might be getting pregnant and what happened to them. I never saw pregnant students on campus. Where were they? When I started researching, I discovered that in the previous year, the Arthur Ashe Student Health and Wellness Center on campus processed more than two thousand pregnancy tests.[5] This same article on "pregnancy counseling" made no reference to any resources for pregnant or parenting students or alternatives to abortion. The only options discussed were referrals for "psychological counseling or pregnancy termination."

As to counseling, the advice offered by the nurse of Women's Health Services was this: "It's okay to regret; it's okay to feel sorry. . . . I just don't want them to beat themselves up about it in the future." The "it" was shorthand for abortion. I could find no information at the center about resources for pregnant students beyond abortion, and no resources for parenting or adoption.

I wasn't sure what to do with the information I was discovering about UCLA's pro-abortion bias, but I knew that in order to make an impact at school, I needed to get more involved in campus activities. I was also eager to make friends, make an impact, and explore what UCLA had to offer. I rushed a sorority (which I joined and then left after six months), ran pro-life meetings, scheduled speakers, visited a dozen different campus groups, and wrote for the campus paper, the *Daily Bruin*. For all that intentional exploration, the event that set me on a new path was unexpected.

One Saturday, I grabbed a to-go salad on my way back to campus after doing some volunteer work at a nearby pregnancy resource center that morning. I was running late for a workshop sponsored by a group called the Leadership Institute, a conservative organization based out of Washington, DC. I took a seat in the back, discreetly ate my salad, and watched a tall young man, overdressed in slacks and a button-down shirt, make a surprisingly dynamic presentation on student journalism. I say surprising because there were only about half-a-dozen libertarians and young Republicans there to listen to the talk in a grungy dorm rec area. I wasn't even sure if I was Republican myself, but I was pro-life and socially conservative, and Republicans accepted these views much more readily than Democrats. The speaker happened to be James O'Keefe, then a recent college graduate who was working for the Leadership Institute and who, years later, would establish his own activist organization.

What I liked about James was his spunk. Passionate and idealistic, James was fresh out of Rutgers University and determined to change the world. He and I became friends, bonding over our shared commitment to the kind of activism that could make a difference. I explained to him my goal of helping educate fellow students about abortion, especially in light of the fact that UCLA had no pro-life resources for pregnant students. I confessed, though, that I did not know where to begin. The *Daily Bruin* would only publish so many pro-life articles, and I wanted to start an independent magazine. But I wasn't sure how to report on the problems I was seeing on campus.

"Why don't you just investigate the health center yourself?" James asked.

It was a great question, albeit a daunting one. I've always loved to act. A natural-born empath, I often imagine and even feel what others might be feeling. Acting is an opportunity to step inside another person's experience and try to feel everything they do. It's been an outlet for me since I was a young girl, from nativity plays at church to competing in dramatic interpretation events in high school. I would eventually even join the mock trial team at UCLA and play a witness—a social worker infected by a client's HIV needle.

Acting was one of my gifts. Here was a chance to use it. James and I came up with a plan to find out what the health center was actually telling students who might be pregnant. I would visit the health center as myself, a student, using my campus ID (all easy enough!), but say that I might be pregnant and needed help. Would they be able to help me? What would they say?

According to plan, James and I walked into the Ashe Center. I showed my ID and asked to speak with a nurse privately. I felt oddly calm. My sense of purpose overcame any discomfort I felt.

Of course, I wasn't pregnant, and James wasn't even a student, but I wasn't about to share either fact with the center staff.

The nurse brought James and me into a private room, and we sat down. I explained that I might be pregnant, and James was my friend, there for moral support. Unsurprisingly, the nurse's goals did not include helping me care for a preborn child. Instead, her goal—I realized quickly—was to encourage me to have an abortion.

"UCLA doesn't support women who are pregnant or help them necessarily," the nurse said flatly.

When I asked what other options I had as a pregnant student, she said that carrying the pregnancy to term on campus would be embarrassing to me and my fellow classmates because I might need to use the bathroom during class. When I asked about adoption, she discouraged it, explaining it would be like "giving away a present." Nothing was said about the fact that this beautiful act of sacrificial love would mean that a child could live rather than die.

For this nurse, the center's idea of "health and wellness" was abortion. She explained that she could refer me to two UCLA doctors who could do an abortion. Better still, they might even find a way to use state Medicaid funds to pay for the abortion so the charge wouldn't show up on my parents' insurance. We left shortly after that.

With a $1,000 grant from the Leadership Institute, Live Action UCLA created a magazine called *The Advocate*. In its initial issue, we published the story of our encounter at the health center and distributed several thousand copies around campus with the headline, "Where Have All the Pregnant Women Gone?" This was my first real plunge into independent media, the battleground for much of my future pro-life activism. The people at the health center were not pleased.

My team members and I used the article as an opportunity to ask for meetings with university administrators. Our goal was to persuade UCLA to give a voice to those promoting alternatives to abortion. We had mixed results. Several administrators met with us. None denied the legitimacy of our request or explicitly stated that pregnant students shouldn't have options, but no one wanted to upset the campus status quo by changing anything.

We also asked to meet with the nurse, and I was surprised when she agreed. Even though I was visiting her undercover when we first met, I felt a strong connection with her, and so I wrestled with what I should say when we met again. I thought that perhaps she didn't realize the harm she was doing. I hoped that maybe she would begin to see the lack of justice and compassion in her pro-abortion stance.

Unfortunately, that did not happen. She seemed totally shut off to the pro-life perspective. She stood by everything she had said in our first meeting, but she also claimed that I had represented her inaccurately.

"How so?" I asked her. "What did I write about you that was inaccurate?" She wouldn't answer and changed the subject to discuss my agenda. Of course, I had an agenda, I tried to explain, and it was this: No child should be dehumanized, destroyed, and discarded. No woman should be told that there is no one to help her carry her baby and care for her newborn. All women should be encouraged to embrace their children, not to abort them. But I felt as if she did not hear what I was saying.

This second meeting with the nurse disturbed me as much as the first. I was grieved when I walked out of the clinic because, despite our conversation, she seemed unmoved. Still, Live Action UCLA had made waves, starting a much-needed conversation on campus about the lack of pregnancy resources at UCLA.

When I first met James O'Keefe, he had no particular interest in abortion as a cause. However, James quickly came to see that no other cause was its equal. He made a great ally because for him nothing was impossible. He had a vision. He believed we really could change the world. I believed that, too, but until I met James, I hadn't translated that belief into independent reporting. As I was learning, there was value in surrounding myself with people who could push me beyond what I thought were my limits.

Another person who influenced both James and me was Mark Crutcher, arguably one of America's most effective pro-life activists. Mark is the head of Life Dynamics, a pro-life advocacy organization based in Denton, Texas. A former car dealer and a born innovator, Mark has been pioneering pro-life strategies since 1992, when he sold his car dealership and launched Life Dynamics from his living room.

When I first met Mark in 2007, he was (and still is) bald, bespectacled, and built like a barrel. Pushing sixty at the time, Mark loved to talk about pro-life strategy and peppered his always colorful language with regionalisms about "West Texas rattlesnakes" and the like that no Californian could ever hope to imitate. A lover of history, Mark knew the background of the abortion industry better than anyone. When I called him for advice, he never failed to provide it no matter how busy he was—and he was always busy.

It was Mark who effectively introduced undercover work to the pro-life movement. In 2000, Mark hired a young woman to pose as a thirteen-year-old girl. Over the course of the next two years, she called more than eight hundred Planned Parenthood facilities across the country. Not all these facilities performed abortions, but those that didn't were happy to make referrals.

On each call, the actor shared her story with a relevant Planned Parenthood staffer, explaining that although she was only thirteen, her boyfriend was much older. In 91 percent of the recorded responses, the staffer she spoke with said something along the lines of, "We won't tell if you don't tell." Despite the fact that Planned Parenthood staff are mandated by law to report suspected statutory rape, they repeatedly told a caller who claimed to be a minor that they wouldn't ask any questions about her much older boyfriend. In other words, these staffers were more than willing to overlook statutory rape. Even more chilling, they were prepared to help dispose of the evidence of the crime, the baby.

I had already investigated UCLA's health center and written about my university's lack of pregnancy resources and promotion of abortion. As I learned about Mark's research, I also discovered that there were several court cases that documented the plights of young pregnant girls who had endured sexual abuse cover-up at Planned Parenthood abortion facilities. Was this happening in the Los Angeles facilities? James and I decided to investigate two clinics just miles away from UCLA to find out how they responded to purported victims of statutory rape. Would they file the mandated report, or would they turn a blind eye?

On a sunny afternoon in March, we made our way to Santa Monica, the location of my first undercover investigation into an abortion facility. This clinic offered referrals for surgical abortions and did chemical abortions on site. For the chemical abortions, staffers gave women two pills. The first pill starved a developing child of nutrients. The second pill induced a miscarriage.

The Planned Parenthood clinic was on the second story of a building it shared with a Coffee Bean café and a women's workout apparel store. I got on the elevator, my heart beating rapidly. In fact, the voice recorder under my shirt picked up the sound of my heartbeat, a kind of background music to what I would record in that clinic. A camcorder I had borrowed from a friend was positioned inside my purse. It was a very low-budget student investigation—or, I should I say, a no-budget student investigation.

I had never been inside an abortion facility before. Would the staffers know I was secretly filming? Would there be a metal detector or some kind of pat-me-down that would reveal the recorder? I was posing as a fifteen-year-old girl, pregnant and frightened, the victim of an older man. In California, any health worker is required by law to report suspected child abuse of minors fifteen and younger. Wearing flip-flops, jeans, and an old T-shirt, I was petite enough, and looked youthful enough at eighteen to pass for fifteen.

The elevator doors opened and I was buzzed in. After entering, I paused in the hallway, looking through a glass door in the clinic waiting room. A brightly colored wall had the word *Esperanza*, "hope" in English, written in large bold letters. However, a more appropriate hope quote would be the one that greeted visitors to Dante's *Inferno*, "Abandon hope all ye who enter here."

I stared at the women clustered in the waiting room, realizing that many were there for an abortion. I knew that each woman represented *two* lives. Within these clinic walls, one of those lives would soon be cruelly destroyed. The only hope offered here was a false one. Authentic and lasting hope cannot be won by ending the life of a child.

From behind the check-in counter, a female Planned Parenthood counselor greeted me. Her response to my scenario would quickly corroborate what Mark Crutcher had documented years ago. I recorded the following exchange on a hidden camera.

"He's twenty-three, and . . . um . . . I am fifteen. Do I have to report that?" I asked hesitantly.

"It depends on how old you are. Let me double-check that," said the counselor. She apparently went to talk to a supervisor and came back a moment or two later.

"If you're fifteen, we have to report that. If not, if you're older than that, we don't need to," she told me.

"But if I just say that I'm *not* fifteen, then it's different?" I asked.

"That's correct," she said.

"So, if I say . . ."

"You could say sixteen."

"Okay," I answered, "so I say 'sixteen.' Okay, so I could just write, I could just write that I'm sixteen?"

"Figure out a birthday that works," said the counselor in a line right out of a movie, "and I don't know anything."

I repeated the strategy later that day at another Planned Parenthood clinic in Los Angeles. The manager sat me down and gave me her advice: "You're talking to someone that had a child at seventeen. It wasn't easy. If I could do it again, I would have done it very differently. . . . If I could do it again, oh, I would not continue the pregnancy. And I have two kids, sixteen and twelve." I wondered if her sixteen-year-old knew how his mother felt about his birth.

I would learn in later years that other Planned Parenthood staff made similar comments as a kind of sales pitch during counseling sessions. A counselor would refer to a past abortion she'd had—or to an abortion she *wished* she'd had—as a way to encourage a hesitant potential client to go ahead and have an abortion. I would also learn that, for some women, working in the abortion industry was a way to deal with the pain of their own abortions. By encouraging other women to abort, they justified their own past choices.

After the two visits, James and I created a video out of the footage and posted it on YouTube, a video-sharing platform that had launched a year or so earlier. Between classes, I pulled up the video to check the number of views as a way to procrastinate doing homework. The numbers slowly climbed the first few hours to one hundred views. They were probably all either from me reloading the page or from my mother reloading it to share with friends in San Jose. Several hours later, though, the view count shot up to one thousand. That number couldn't possibly have been from me and my mom. I was thrilled—we were going viral on YouTube! The next day, several blogs had picked up the video and the view count shot to twenty thousand. I was blown away. Never in my most ambitious dreams had I imagined our little video would be viewed by twenty thousand people. (Over a decade later, Live Action would celebrate achieving a combined billion views of our video content!)

Not too long after we posted the video on YouTube, I sat down at my dorm room desk to check my messages and found an e-mail from Planned Parenthood. I remember wondering how I got on their LISTSERV. Was this some sort of sick joke?

Little did I know that this would not be my last correspondence with the nation's largest abortion provider.

> Dear Ms. Rose . . . PPLA recently became aware of two videos you posted on YouTube.com of excerpts of conversations with Planned Parenthood employees. . . . You have violated the privacy of PPLA employees. . . . If you do not remove those videos from YouTube, as well as relinquish all the tapes of those conversations to Planned Parenthood, you are subject to fines of $5,000 for each offense and PPLA will seek a full range of civil and legal remedies against you, . . . without any additional warning to you.

This friendly little threat was signed by Mary Jane Wagle, president and CEO of Planned Parenthood Los Angeles. I remember staring wide-eyed at my computer, startled by the realization that Planned Parenthood, the billion-dollar corporation and number one provider of abortions in America, was afraid—afraid of the story our videos told, afraid of the truth our videos revealed. Planned Parenthood's clinics were blatantly violating California's mandatory reporting laws for sexual abuse. The problem was that this time they got caught.

I had less than a few hundred dollars in my bank account at the time, so good luck with that, Planned Parenthood. As I sat at my desk after getting that e-mail, I didn't know exactly what to do next, except to pray. So I got on my knees in my dorm room and prayed, "God, use me. Use this to help save lives."

Within twenty-four hours I was connected with the Alliance Defense Fund (ADF). This organization provides pro-bono legal advice for college students facing threats to their free speech or, in this case, their efforts at citizen journalism. I also started getting dozens of calls from media outlets, including TV stations. I was asked to make my first-ever TV appearance on what just happened to be at the time the highest-rated show on cable news.

I spent hours going over my talking points for the interview with my dedicated ADF attorney, David French. My goal was to say what I had documented at the facility and explain that this was part of a systemic problem at Planned Parenthood. The two facilities I visited were clearly not the only ones covering up sexual abuse.

The day of the interview I was too excited to even feel anxious. I didn't have any professional clothes, but I found a black top that looked fancy enough. On schedule, a black limo arrived outside my dorm to take me to a studio about twenty minutes away. The Fox News host would interview me from New York. I would be doing what they call a remote.

Upon arrival at the Los Angeles studio, I was escorted to the green room where I nervously awaited my interview. A green room sounded very official to me, especially after the limo, so I wondered if there would be any free snacks or treats there. Too bad—there was only a water cooler. Unusual for Fox, too, there was no one available to apply TV makeup, so I ended up looking even younger on screen than I did in real life, like an actual fifteen-year-old.

At the time, however, I wasn't thinking about how I looked or even what I would say. I was just thrilled realizing that the very video footage that Planned Parenthood was trying to get deleted from YouTube would be aired on the show for millions of people to see. Planned Parenthood's threat to sue me is what had caught the attention of the news media. Had Planned Parenthood just ignored me, the videos might never have gotten beyond YouTube. The abortion group would drop their lawsuit threat against me: it had become more trouble than it was worth.

I had no idea at the time how this first investigation into Planned Parenthood, the lawsuit threat, and the subsequent media coverage would shape the next fifteen years of my life. I did learn, however, that if I were willing to leave my comfort zone, if I tried the unconventional and took risks, my efforts might be rewarded in ways beyond what I could ever have anticipated.

■

There was never a perfect time to take the next step in my advocacy work. The resources were never perfectly lined up. There were always good reasons to *not* take action. I was a student after all. Maybe, I thought, I should stick to my studies and focus on getting straight As. Maybe I shouldn't attempt student reporting without formal journalism training. Maybe I risked expulsion by exposing my own school's leadership. No decision I made was free of risk.

I didn't have all the steps mapped out, but leaving my comfort zone had launched me on a trajectory that would dramatically alter my future work. Along the way, I learned an essential lesson of leadership: some risk is necessary if you want to force change.

There will always be a thousand reasons not to do something risky, and even more to continue doing what is familiar and comfortable. Creation is hard. Activism is hard. Doing anything controversial, unusual, unpopular, is hard.

It will always be easier to sit in silence than to speak up for what is right. Why?

You and I are not robots or animals. We have free will and, given our wounded human nature, there are often times we choose to be diverted. It seems clear to me, too, that there are evil forces pushing back against any good endeavor. I also believe there are demonic roadblocks stopping us from standing for what is right and good and loving. Evil exists, and Satan's only intent is to destroy and kill. He hates all creation. He hates all truth. He hates anything that has life and breath. Evil depends on our apathy, our lukewarmness, our attachment to the safe, the familiar, the comfortable.

Every day we are up against forces that do not want us to live out our God-given potential. Those forces do not want us to love. Those forces do not want us to create. Those forces do not want us to explore and discover and use the unique talents we have to make a difference in the world. As a voice of inspiration tells us to just start, the voice of opposition whispers a thousand reasons to sit and do nothing instead.

Love of the comfortable or familiar can end our work before it has even begun. We have to ask ourselves: How badly do I want to change the world? How badly do I want to make a difference? Allowing our hearts to feel the pain of those we seek to help, or admiring the heroes who have gone before us, can help shake us from our lethargy. Focusing on those children in danger of death and the possibility that I could help them is what gave me the courage to go undercover and take risks that I could very well have chosen to avoid.

If I had, instead, focused my energies on understanding all the ramifications of doing pro-life work at UCLA before I got started, I might have been overwhelmed. This doesn't mean we should never evaluate or weigh risks in advance, but it does mean that we should not allow ourselves to become stuck in the familiar simply because it is comfortable. We will never build resilience by staying in our comfort zone. We cannot change the world by avoiding its mess and complications. Risk is necessary.

And even though it can seem scary at first, the good news is that taking risks is usually easier to do in reality than in our own minds, where we may lose momentum by imagining worst-case scenarios or talking ourselves out of taking a stand for what is right. God gives each of us grace in the present moment, not in the countless future scenarios we may drum up in our imaginations. Be encouraged that leaving your comfort zone can be as simple as making a decision today to break out of your routine, out of doing only what is comfortable, easy, or familiar, and trying something that is more difficult, daring, or unfamiliar in service of others. When we dare to do what is right or good or loving, God can take our imperfect actions and bring good from them. Saint Augustine said, "God provides the wind, but man must raise the sails."

CHAPTER 10

Build a Team

At the beginning of my lifetime battle against Planned Parenthood, this behemoth had what you might call a financial edge: roughly $1.3 billion in annual revenue compared to Live Action's nearly zero dollars in annual revenue. At the time, roughly half of Planned Parenthood's $1.3 billion budget was provided by taxpayers. I knew I would need all the help I could get. I needed a team.

I was eager to take our undercover investigations to other states to show that abuses in the abortion industry were not limited to a couple of Los Angeles–area clinics. From Mark Crutcher's exposé of more than eight hundred Planned Parenthood facilities, and from court cases documenting how young girls had endured sexual abuse cover-up at abortion clinics, we had reason to believe that abortion clinics nationwide were turning a blind eye to statutory rape and that Planned Parenthood was the greatest offender of them all.

Hundreds of underage young girls were getting abortions every day, many at Planned Parenthood clinics. We knew from Crutcher's work that the clinics, having disposed of the "evidence," had few scruples about sending these girls back to the arms of their abusers—older boyfriends, stepfathers, mothers' boyfriends.

Although I was busy with school and Live Action UCLA, I knew I had to do something more. There was little to no media coverage of the abortion industry and even fewer critical stories. Although mainstream reporters did exposés on everything from the dairy industry to the treatment of restaurant workers, abortion clinics were rarely investigated. Yet, Planned Parenthood was in all our communities, receiving hundreds of millions of dollars from taxpayers, harming countless girls, and killing hundreds of thousands of babies every year.

With the help of two friends, I began to brainstorm a larger plan: going across the country to investigate clinics during my summer break following my sophomore year. I knew such an investigation was possible, but it would cost money we did not have. To get started, I put together a budget, including travel costs for a three-week investigation, per diems for the small team that would be on the road with me, a modest research budget, and equipment I thought we'd need. The total came to about $40,000.

Although I was still a novice in team building, I knew we needed to build a strong one. When I started Live Action, my goal was to develop an organization bigger than myself. In the classic book *The Art of War*, Chinese General Sun Tzu argued that the winner of the battle will be the general "whose army is animated by the same spirit throughout all its ranks."[1] I needed to find animated teammates who, like me, were passionate about ending abortion and building a culture of life.

Teams are powerful. As the African proverb says, "If you want to go fast, go it alone. If you want to go far, go together." Although individual initiative is critical, leaders grow their organizations by surrounding themselves with talented, driven people who share their goals. Steve Jobs needed Steve Wozniak. Bill Gates needed Paul Allen. Paul McCartney needed John, George, and Ringo.

Social reform movements also require teamwork. The goal of a movement is to make change. To do this, someone has to persuade people that change is needed. Persuasion is most powerful when many voices endorse—from their own unique experiences—the necessity of a given action. Leaders cultivate these voices by investing in the formation of those on their teams, knowing that they, too, have the capacity to influence others.

There's a popular TED Talk called "How to Start a Movement" by writer and entrepreneur Derek Sivers. Sivers used a funny video to illustrate how to draw people into a movement. The video shows a young man who begins to dance freely in public. His actions inspire another person to dance alongside him. As Sivers observed, "The first follower is what transforms a lone nut into a leader."[2] Indeed, after one follower becomes two, and two become three, it isn't long before dozens of people are dancing.

A similar principle applies to the history of social reform. By taking bold actions, leaders create a path for others to follow. Those followers, in turn, persuade other people to join them. Not even the greatest leaders of social reform, such as William Wilberforce, Martin Luther King, or Mother Teresa, could have succeeded alone. Powerful orators and activists, King and Wilberforce used their words to inspire people to action. The soft-spoken Mother Teresa inspired people through both her profound words and her example. Leaders of social movements are effective only to the degree that they persuade others to join them in their causes. If would-be leaders do not learn to work with other people to accomplish their goals, they will not become leaders.

Any team is larger than the full-time players. At UCLA, for instance, a dozen athletes play on the men's basketball team, but the larger team also includes the coaches and the trainers. A case could also be made that the marketers, the family members, the students, the alumni, the fans, and the boosters are part of the team as well. It is up to the players to work in harmony to win the game, but the larger community provides the support, the guidance, and, ideally, the funding that enables the athletes to play well.

To hire an investigative team I needed money, and I realized that no one would contribute to our mission unless we asked. I knew that if Live Action had the resources to travel nationally and document how abortion facilities covered up statutory rape, we might be able to raise awareness about abortion in a way that had not happened before. On the basis of that awareness, we could build enough political pressure to end public funding of the abortion industry.

It was clear that our next step was fundraising, but we also faced an unusual obstacle in that regard. In order for our efforts to succeed, we had to keep them a secret. I needed to somehow raise $40,000 to cover the cost of the investigation while telling almost no one what the funds were for.

Fortunately, providence was at work. A few weeks prior to our brain-storming session, I had met with a potential donor named Larry, a very tall man with a kind face, at a speaking event in Washington, DC, that I had been invited to after one of its organizers heard a radio interview I had done. We exchanged business cards, and he told me they would be happy to help me if they could. I didn't know exactly what form that help might take, but I learned he was a board member for several other nonprofits and was very generous. He also lived in Southern California, an hour from UCLA.

Lacking any formal training in sales or fundraising, I read every fundraising book I could get my hands on and researched online how to make an ask. I put together a written proposal and put the budget in a for-mat that I thought looked professional. Even though I would be sharing the proposal only with a handful of potential supporters, I kept much of the information vague. We could not risk a leak to the opposition.

Once the proposal was completed, I e-mailed the donor and asked if we could meet. He agreed and said he would put together a luncheon and recruit some friends who he often teamed up with to sponsor good causes. He suggested we all meet at a country club in Orange County. Having no car, I asked Christina, my curly-haired and ever-loyal room-mate, friend, and fellow pro-life activist, to drive with me to the meeting on the following Saturday and be my wingwoman at the lunch. She was my core team, and this would be one of many escapades throughout college that Christina made possible with her unflagging support.

The potential donor had said the dress code was "Newport casual" and that we would be having lunch. I knew jeans were out of the question, but otherwise I had no idea what "Newport casual" meant. Having been the girl in high school who loved shopping at thrift stores, I was at a loss. I tended to improvise outfits that weren't necessarily fashionable but that I found eclectic and cute. I liked patterned tank tops, oversized jackets, and bohemian-style dresses. As a student at UCLA, my clothes blended in well enough with the other forty thousand varieties of preppy, alternative, grunge, fast fashion, and other styles found on campus.

But when it came to a fancy donor lunch? Doing a TV interview? Giving a speech at a political event in Washington, DC, where I was the youngest person by at least twenty years? It was hard to know where to start. In high school, I had to dress for speech and debate tournaments, but the black slacks, striped button-ups, and ties I wore to those events had long ago been donated to Goodwill.

The week before the meeting, I went through my closet trying to find a suitable outfit. No luck. I had no casual business clothes, just a long-sleeved, heavy knit black dress from Ann Taylor Loft that felt more appropriate for an East Coast funeral than a spring lunch at a Southern California country club. Plus, it made me appear as if I were trying to look twice my age.

Christina's older sister ran her own company and had grown-up clothes. She gave us permission to look through her closet to see if there was anything appropriate that fit me, but everything was either too big or too long. Being busy all week with classes and homework, we didn't have time before Saturday to shop. Instead, we decided to wait until Saturday morning before the lunch to find our outfits. I'd bring the black dress along as a backup.

That Saturday morning, we got an early start at Target, hoping to find something inexpensive but cute that somehow said "country club casual." I didn't really have any money to be spending on clothes, but that didn't matter to me. I was ready to spend my last red cent on this opportunity. Hustling through each aisle of the women's section, I finally found a white-and-black striped dress, a pair of heeled sandals, and a matching purse made of faux straw that looked beachy but classy.

One hundred and thirteen dollars later, I headed to the Target restroom to get dressed in my new outfit, leaving the tags hidden underneath the dress because I didn't have scissors to cut them off. Mission accomplished, we drove to a Kinkos to print out our presentation materials and made it to the country club parking lot minutes before our scheduled lunch.

We carefully cruised past a BMW, an Escalade, and a gleaming red Ferrari. I motioned for Christina to keep driving straight to the very back of the lot, despite the ample open spots up close. We parked her beat-up Toyota next to a hedge. Before exiting, I opened the book *Making the Ask* to remind myself of one of the core lessons of asking: Once you've discussed your goal and confirmed the donor's excitement about it, simply state what the project will cost and ask them to help you accomplish it. And then be quiet. Let there be an awkward pause, if necessary, but allow the donor to speak next. That silence is necessary to get the donor to commit. If the would-be donor does not commit at the meeting, it would be much harder to get a commitment later.

A little nervous, Christina and I walked into the country club. The lobby floor gleamed, but the gourmet chocolates wrapped in luxurious foil sitting in a crystal bowl on the beautiful walnut-stained check-in counter caught my eye. Always on the hunt for treats, I made a mental note to snag a few on the way out.

We gave the name of our host at the front desk and were escorted to a private room where several couples waited to greet us. I said hello to Larry, whom I had met in Washington, and he introduced us to his wife, Margie, a soft-spoken woman with a beautiful smile, and to his group of welcoming and well-heeled friends. One woman particularly impressed me. Beautifully dressed, she wore multiple strands of sparkling necklaces and had bright blue eyes and a warm, inviting expression. If Orange County had a queen, she would have been a leading candidate for the role. Later, both the tall donor and his wife and this elegant woman, Kim, and her husband, Tom, would become my dear friends, but at the moment, I quietly thanked God that I was wearing a short sleeve, light-colored poplin dress and not a black one fit for a funeral.

We sat down for lunch. While Christina and I awkwardly picked at our tuna Niçoise salads, these very nice people asked about our activism, our school, and our families. After forty-five minutes of small talk, I wondered when, or if, I would get to hand out my plans and make the Big Ask. I grew increasingly nervous. Maybe I had misunderstood the donor's intention and he and his friends wouldn't be donors after all. Maybe I should have just ordered the hamburger.

One of the hosts, a businessman in a well-tailored suit, took the lead. He suddenly stopped the chit-chat and said to me, "Okay, what do you want to do?"

With adrenaline kicking in for the big pitch, I started explaining our goal. I told him and the others how we could help change the national conversation on abortion if we could expose the many abuses of Planned Parenthood, starting with their cover-up of statutory rape. I expressed my confidence that we could get the evidence in just a few weeks if we had the resources to assemble a team. I kept talking and talking, feeling more and more nervous by the minute. All the while I was thinking, *Should I keep talking? When exactly do I ask for the money?* I handed out the flyers and kept talking, detailing my plans and justifying my budget. In my nervousness, I forgot to make the dramatic pause I had practiced. I just kept talking.

Finally, the businessman interrupted me. "Lila, Lila, we get it. You don't need to keep talking. We're gonna give you the money."

A lump grew in my throat, and I almost burst into tears. It seemed too good to be true. Looking back, I see how generous and patient our hosts were. I also realize how amateurish my efforts were. A dozen or so years later, these donors have become friends and comrades, key members of our team. I've come to believe that when people want to give, they give! They need to be offered the opportunity and have that opportunity explained, but the most enduring supporters will be those who are all-in.

Even so, selling them a big idea and then pressuring them to donate at a lunch or dinner is not a useful long-term strategy. Some fundraising experts may disagree because they think a hard sell is just as viable for a nonprofit as it is for, say, a car dealership. But I have not found high-pressure tactics to be effective over the long term.

I would learn later how each of these generous people had been dedicated to the fight for life and family for years, and they were eager to encourage a new generation of activists. Seeing how passionate I was to make a change in a world where so few changes had been made, they wanted to help. They were willing to take a risk on a bold plan with a nineteen-year-old girl who had little experience but lots of nerve.

Whatever cause you are fighting for, there will be others out there who agree with you and want to help. It's likely they have been working to solve the same problem or a similar one, and it's possible they started that work long before you did. Finding them is key. To fight a leviathan takes a team. And it can take a lot of trial and error to build a team.

Thanks to our donors from the country club, Christina and I had already raised the $40,000 we needed. Now it was time to put together a road team to go beyond California and expose the fact that Planned Parenthood's sexual abuse cover-up wasn't limited to two Los Angeles abortion clinics.

I started going through a list of my high school friends in my mind, thinking through which ones might be interested in helping. Were they already committed to the pro-life cause, or if they weren't, would they be willing to get involved? I also thought about what gifts my friends had and how they might contribute to our mission. Eventually, a childhood friend who had a talent for acting agreed to come with me to pose as another underage girl. Another gifted friend who had a passion for film-making agreed to be our cameraman.

We still needed a trip lead, someone to drive, manage logistics, and handle the equipment. The lead needed to be discreet, detail-oriented, trustworthy, and old enough to have car insurance, which was twenty-five in California. That person also had to be able to take three weeks off with little pay. Oh, and they had to be willing to keep what they were doing a secret from their family and friends.

I spent weeks calling friends and asking if they knew anyone will-ing to spend three weeks of their summer on a "special film project." I could find no one. I interviewed a few prospects by phone, but none were quite right. Some needed more money. Others were not available during the dates we needed them or were uncomfortable doing something they couldn't talk about.

I was purposely vague with everyone I contacted. I did not share any details of what we planned to do and did not even mention the undercover nature of the project. I knew that if I found a candidate I really liked, I would tell them a little more, gauge their interest, and then have them sign a nondisclosure agreement before sharing the details. I had spent months studying Mark Crutcher's work, the work of other investigative journalists, and had even dabbled in private investigator training to learn techniques to use. I improvised as I went.

I anxiously paced the patio in my parents' backyard as I made my calls. One person I called was Jonathan Keller, the trustworthy Fresno pro-life leader and mentor who had helped me start Live Action in high school. When I explained what we were looking for, he did not hesitate to suggest likely candidates. Then, halfway through each suggestion, he would think of a reason that person wasn't right and stop himself. "Oh, no, I forgot, they're getting married then!" Or, "Actually, nah, that won't work. I don't even know how pro-life they are."

"Is there anyone else at all you can think of?" I asked.

"I don't think so," he said. "I'm sorry."

Later, a friend came by and was doing summer school homework at our kitchen table when I poured out my frustration. "I don't know what to do," I fretted. "We are supposed to leave for this trip in five days, and I still haven't found the trip lead."

"Don't worry, Lila," my friend assured me. "It will work out. Trust God."

"You're right," I said. "If this project is supposed to happen, the pieces will fall into place."

A few minutes later, my phone rang. It was Jonathan.

"Hey! I just thought of one more person," he said.

As he described his friend, relief flooded over me. David Martin sounded like an answered prayer. Within hours, I was on the phone with David, and the next day, he drove several hours to my parents' house to meet me in person and work through the itinerary. We were ready to go, but not even our parents knew where we were going or what exactly we were doing.

It is one thing to build a team; it is another challenge to make that team work. A healthy team requires its members to appreciate what every other team member has to offer. Members need to appreciate their own talents while simultaneously having the humility to use those talents in service of the best interests of the team. They also need to be willing to have hard conversations when needed and to be accountable to one another.

To work in harmony, team members have to resist the temptation to play to the crowd. Recognition and applause may stoke the ego, but they are never as satisfying as shared wins. But you can't have shared wins if you are possessive about the work you are doing and unwilling to invite other people into it. One of the hardest lessons I've learned again and again over the years is the power of delegation and shared responsibility.

As leaders, we may sometimes think that we have to own both the problem and the solution ourselves, that we have to work harder than anyone and prove ourselves worthy of leading by being the best. While it is important to set the example by working hard and striving every day for excellence, our job as leaders is not to prove to our team that we are the best, but to help our team improve so that we can all excel together. No one of us are the best at everything; that's impossible. We need each other and the unique gifts and strengths that others have, which are different from our own. Over the years, Live Action has recruited extremely talented writers, video producers, and researchers who shine in their unique creative expertise.

Identifying our own weaknesses or challenges as leaders is also key, because it is precisely in the areas where we fall short that we can recruit others who shine. Live Action would have never achieved all its impact over the years if I had tried to go it alone, or if I failed to tap into the great strengths of my team members and delegate huge portions of the work to them. I've worked with Lauren, Live Action's head of development, for more than six years, and she's helped sustain the dramatic growth of our organization's fundraising and team. Driven to become her best in personnel management and health, Lauren's consistent, patient management skills have been a crucial complement to my intense vision casting. Today, Live Action's lifesaving work is the hard-won outcome of people like Lauren giving it their all. By doing the difficult daily work of figuring out how to understand one another, collaborate, and lean in to our individual roles on our team, we can push forward to victory.

One of the unique challenges for our Mona Lisa project was developing undercover personas. My persona was especially tricky, since Planned Parenthood essentially put up a wanted poster after my California investigation, warning staff to be on the lookout for yours truly. On a scouting visit to a Planned Parenthood, one of our team members spotted the poster on the bulletin board behind the front desk with my picture on it and took it down when no one was looking. I laughed when I saw it. The poster included a screenshot of me from a TV interview and claimed I was last seen in Florida. In fact, I had never stepped foot in Florida, not even for Disney World. Plus, Florida's laws weren't very protective of investigative journalism, making undercover projects difficult.

We decided I needed a disguise—so I agreed to bleach my hair and wear glasses. At the beginning of the trip, we stopped at a CVS. We continued talking through our investigative scenarios as I sat for hours in our hotel room with bleach in my hair, but to no avail. The drugstore bleach wasn't strong enough, and the result was a greenish shade of light brown, not exactly the dramatic change needed for a successful disguise.

Hoping for a better outcome, we headed to a hair salon at a nearby strip mall. While the rest of the team browsed the mall, I sat in a chair for three hours under the florescent salon lights, bleach burning my scalp, this time applied by a professional. She did a good job. Hours later, I was very blonde. Our team would be able to complete the next few weeks of investigative work undetected.

The first stop on our three-week itinerary was Cincinnati, Ohio. Once there, we settled into a local hotel to train for a few days before beginning our undercover work. We spent hours carefully reviewing the briefs we had made. We laid out all our undercover equipment on the floor and organized it carefully, charging batteries and sewing cameras into clothes and purses. We studied the facilities we would be investigating and practiced our undercover personas. We also talked about our fears or concerns and spent time troubleshooting scenarios of what might go wrong or conflicts we may have. Soon enough, all our work, all our planning and preparation, would be put to the test.

CHAPTER 11

Expose the Evil

Looking for inspiration for the Mona Lisa project, I had planned a visit for our small team to the National Underground Railroad Freedom Center in Cincinnati. The museum exists to raise awareness about our nation's terrible legacy of slavery, racism, and Jim Crow laws. It also honors the work of the abolitionists and civil rights movement heroes who have fought and sacrificed for justice.

The museum included replicas of the instruments used to imprison Blacks: handcuffs, cages, restraining bars for the shoulders and arms. We walked quietly through the exhibits that detailed the lynching, enslavement, and dehumanizing horrors of the transatlantic slave trade. Brutal slave traders had locked helpless men, women, and children into coffin-like boxes on ships, giving them little food or water for weeks and leaving many to die in their own vomit and excrement.

It was astonishing to think that less than two centuries ago in the United States, everyday people from both the North and the South accepted slavery as a normal institution, a part of daily life, many without questioning it. Throughout most of human history, slavery had been accepted as a normal practice. Many Americans participated directly in the cruelties that so many Blacks endured: excruciating family separations, rapes, physical torture and abuse, the parading of naked human beings at markets where they were bought and sold as livestock.

As I read the stories and saw the displays, I tried to come to terms with the willingness of everyday people to participate in such an evil institution. *How could any human being buy or sell other humans and treat them like cattle?* I had asked similar questions years earlier when reading about the Holocaust. *How could anyone send a little child into a gas chamber? How could anyone shoot a mother in the head, in front of her children no less?*

The common theme, I learned, was dehumanization. The groundwork for the Holocaust was established long before the concentration camps were constructed. In his landmark book, *Nazi Germany and the Jews*, Saul Friedländer, a Holocaust survivor and a professor of mine at UCLA, argued that, yes, "ordinary people" living in a modern society not unlike our own perpetrated these horrors. He did not mean that ordinary people were intrinsically evil. What he meant was that ordinary people, conditioned by "a regime, an ideology, and a political culture that were anything but commonplace,"[1] could do terribly evil things if the evil seemed *normal*.

In that sense, what happened in Nazi Germany in the mid-twentieth century was horrific but not exceptional. The National Underground Railroad Freedom Center reminded us that dehumanizing our fellow human beings was not limited to one century or one nation. It was a warning of what could happen any time when we view our brothers and sisters as the other, as less than, and dehumanize them.

How do we combat dehumanization? Successful social reform movements combat it by working to rehumanize the victims of dehumanization. Gregg Cunningham, founder of the Center for Bio-Ethical Reform, an anti-abortion organization, believes that graphic imagery plays a key role in such efforts. Gregg said, "The history of social reform is the history of horrifying pictures."[2] He then cited several examples: "Pictures of Native American women and children massacred by the U.S. Calvary. Pictures of African Americans beaten to their knees for trying to register to vote. Pictures of little children suffering terrible abuses in American coal mines and factories." Such imagery, he contended, "convinced the country that the victims were real people, fully entitled to rights of personhood." The images "also persuaded the electorate that the injustices depicted therein were sufficiently egregious to warrant criminalization."

Under Gregg's leadership, the Center for Bio-Ethical Reform has done painstaking, groundbreaking work to capture images and video of abortion victims. To help convince an unbelieving world, Gregg has also secured signed statements from abortionists verifying that the photos and film footage are authentic.

Vivid images have the power to rehumanize victims, and so we have to be willing to show them. Such images have the power to drive change. Jonathan Klein, cofounder and chairman of Getty Images, has said, "Since the beginning of photography, images have provoked reactions in people, and those reactions have caused change to happen."[3] Images have the power to fuel entire movements that lead to social change. It's a truth that has been demonstrated time and again in many social reform movements over the last century, including the American civil rights movement.

In 1955, fourteen-year-old Emmett Till of Chicago was visiting his cousins in Mississippi. One day, while playing outside a small grocery store, Emmett was accused of whistling at the young female proprietor. A few days later, the woman's husband and his brother abducted Emmett at gunpoint from his elderly uncle's house and beat him brutally, almost beyond recognition. They then shot the young teenager in the head and dumped his body in a river.

The story of his murder spread like wildfire through Chicago's Black community. Distraught, Emmett's mother, Mamie Till Bradley, demanded that she be sent the body of her son so she could bury him in Chicago.

The coroner had sealed the coffin, but Mamie insisted on seeing her precious son before his burial. Looking at his broken, swollen, and disfigured body, she decided to hold a public funeral and leave his casket open. "I wanted the world to see what they did to my baby," she said. Thousands attended the service, and photojournalists took pictures. Once published, these photos shocked the nation as they exposed the brutality of racism. The photos also brought attention to the utter failure of the justice system to protect Blacks: Emmett's killers were acquitted by an all-white jury. Mamie's controversial decision to leave his coffin open helped spark the civil rights movement. Images matter. They can change everything.

As our Mona Lisa team wandered the National Underground Railroad Freedom Center, we contemplated how each century had its own strain of blindness to the humanity of every person. Abortion was our era's great injustice: in America alone, from the time abortion had been legalized to the time we toured the Freedom Center, more than thirty-five million children had been killed.[4] In the few hours we were there, as many as a thousand more children would die in the nation whose taxpayers were funding Planned Parenthood.

In a telling NPR interview, David Livingstone Smith, a professor of philosophy and author of the book *Less Than Human: Why We Demean, Enslave, and Exterminate Others*, explained how societies have dehumanized others to overcome "very deep and natural inhibitions" against killing them. "Thinking sets the agenda for action, and thinking of humans as less than human paves the way for atrocity," wrote Smith in an excerpt from his book. "It's wrong to kill a person, but permissible to exterminate a rat. To the Nazis, all the Jews, Gypsies and others were rats: dangerous, disease-carrying rats."[5]

You might think that Smith would be a champion of the pro-life cause. You would be wrong. In *Less Than Human*, Smith made only one reference to abortion. He spoke of it in reference to the "great chain of being," a hierarchical view of the value of matter and life, which he described as "an ancient, discredited, prescientific model of the cosmos." His point was that our moral judgments about what can and cannot experience harm "depend in large measure on where we place them on the great chain of being." He wrote:

> Intuitions get foggier as we climb higher. Is swatting a mosquito cruel? How about stepping on a cockroach or skewering a writhing worm on a fishhook? Plunging a living lobster into boiling water, or gutting a trout for dinner? Killing a chicken? Slaughtering a lamb? Performing an abortion? Executing a criminal?[6]

Whether consciously or not, Smith found one victim in this chain unworthy of designation even as an object of pity. He spoke of cockroaches, worms, lobsters, and criminals, but when it came to abortion, Smith wrote only, "performing an abortion." He refused to say who or even what it was that was being aborted. In a glaring moral cop-out, he not only dehumanized the baby, but also denied the baby's existence. With this denial, he could ignore the fifty million American babies killed in the forty years prior to the publication of his book and the controversy surrounding their deaths. That an authority on dehumanization such as Smith could overlook the most flagrant example of that very phenomenon is a testament to the abortion industry's lock on the culture. It also serves as a reminder of just how much work those of us in the pro-life movement have left to do.

Today, the most dehumanized among us is the child in the womb. This child is not even considered a human worthy of basic legal protection. Indeed, the unwanted unborn enjoy fewer protections than unwanted animals. Instead, preborn children are routinely dismembered, suctioned to death, deprived of nutrients, or given lethal injections, all with the consent of the law and in the name of "rights."

Education about the humanity of the child is desperately needed. People need to be shown the evil of abortion, the true agenda of abortionists, and the abuses of the abortion industry. Inspired by the abolitionists and civil rights activists, our Mona Lisa team was determined to provide education about what was happening, to make whatever impact we could to put an end to this injustice. Video cameras would be our weapons. Video footage was even more powerful than a single image. We believed that capturing the stories of the abortion industry's abuses on camera and exposing them to the world would put a human face on our campaign for justice.

We set off to begin the investigation. I had stopped at Walmart and bought clothes a thirteen-year-old might wear. *Hannah Montana* was one of the most popular TV shows for middle school students at the time, and so for one of my outfits I bought a colorful T-shirt with Hannah Montana's face on it.

"Guys, I know it's kind of weird," I said, "but I'm going to start acting like a thirteen-year-old for at least the hour before I go into the clinic."

I was sitting in the back of an SUV, dressed up in a pair of old jeans and my Hannah Montana T-shirt. My friend was wearing a sparkly headband and a top from the pre-teen section in Walmart. With our button cameras in place, we started talking like teenage friends. It wasn't that difficult for us. We had been best friends since we were ten and felt at ease with each other. But we needed to get in character.

The roles we would be playing varied dramatically from the real lives we experienced as teens. I was Bri, the thirteen-year-old victim of a sexual abuser who was twice my age. Just nineteen at the time, I could still pass pretty easily for a thirteen-year-old. Clinic staff should recognize my situation as a clear-cut case of statutory rape. By law, they were required to immediately report my case to Child Protective Services or the police.

My friend was Madison, my fifteen-year-old cousin whose family either did not know or care that she was accompanying another underage girl to an abortion clinic. We were visiting Planned Parenthood's Bloomington Health Center, an easy walk from the University of Indiana campus, a little more than two hours due west of Cincinnati. The facility would be one of more than half a dozen we would investigate during our tour. The conversation that follows was recorded and then transcribed word for word.

Counselor: I saw the note that you want to talk about an abortion. Have you had a positive pregnancy test? Okay? And missed a period?

Bri: A couple periods.

Counselor: A couple periods, okay. Okay. How old are you?

Bri: Is that confidential?

Counselor: Yeah, I don't know you from Adam. 'Cause all I have are the first three letters of your name. Bry or Bri.

Bri: Bri.

Counselor: So, I don't know who you are.

Bri: Okay.

Counselor: And our services here are totally confidential anyway. We don't give out anything. No way. That's the way we work here. For everything, abortion, family planning. That's just the way we do it.

Bri: Okay, I'm thirteen.

Counselor: Okay. And go ahead.

Bri: I just need to talk about getting an abortion because my parents . . .

Counselor: Okay. Do you live with a parent?

Bri: I live with her. I mean she's my cousin. I live with her. My parents aren't even here.

Counselor: Where are they?

Bri: In California.

Counselor: Okay, let me just tell you what the problem's going to be. In the state of Indiana, you have to have a parent's signature to get an abortion. One parent.

Bri: I can't. I really can't tell my parents. Because if they found out, they would find out everything.

Counselor: Okay. If you told them, they would find out everything?

Bri: Yeah, I mean they would want to know who was the father and everything, and I can't tell. I wouldn't want to tell them about all that stuff.

Counselor: Okay. Okay.

Bri: He would be in really big trouble.

Counselor: 'Cause I don't want to know how old he is, okay?

Bri: What do you mean?

Counselor: I don't want to know how old he is, okay? Because, in the state of Indiana, [for] anyone thirteen years and younger, there has to be a report done to CPS [Child Protective Services].

Bri: But he's not, he's not as old. I mean he might . . .

Counselor: Doesn't matter.

Bri: . . . be a lot older, but he doesn't act a lot older, you know, and I act a lot older than I am. So it works out because he might be thirty-one. He's older, but, he's not like older. I don't know. You know what I'm talking about?

Madison: But he's not like that. He's not weird or anything.

Bri: Yeah, he's not weird.

Counselor: In the state of Indiana, when anyone has had intercourse, and they're aged thirteen and younger . . .

Bri: I'm almost fourteen.

Counselor: It doesn't matter. You're thirteen. It has to be reported to Child Protective Services. You understand what I'm saying?

Bri: If I got an abortion here, it would have to be reported?

Counselor: Yeah, you know, I can't make you fill out the information with me today. I am supposed to report to Child Protective Services that you are pregnant, and you're thirteen years old. Yes. We have to report that to child protection.

Madison: So how could you do it without, like, having, getting in trouble? 'Cause my parents can't know about it either, but like it's fine, he is a great guy. And . . .

Counselor: Doesn't matter. I know that you're not grasping what I'm saying. Not at all. Because anyone, okay. I didn't hear the age. I don't want to know the age.

Madison: Okay. Great.

Bri: You don't want to know the age?

Counselor: Anyone . . . Let me go get you a chart so that I can explain it fully.

The counselor pauses to get the appropriate chart.

Counselor: Okay, anyone. I know this is a crazy chart. Your age, okay, age of patient, you're thirteen. Okay. So.

Bri: But I'm almost fourteen.

Counselor: Okay, anyone . . .

Bri: I'll be fourteen in like a month and a half.

Counselor: Say you are fourteen, okay. It would not need to be reported to child protection. Okay, if you had an abortion in the state of Indiana.

Bri: So, if I went when I'm fourteen?

Counselor: Yeah, but if you're already two months, you're going to be too far to have an abortion. When was your last period?

Bri: Um, two and a half months or something.

Counselor: March, March, March. Let's just say March 15. You're already twelve weeks. Mmm . . . Anyway, what I'm trying to, let me explain this one part. Then we got to work on this other part. Because you're in between a rock and a hard spot. I mean you really are. I mean we're talking, this is a problem. You need to get this taken care of ASAP. And the problem is, is that you can't get your parents' okay. Anyway, age of patient, say you're fourteen.

The conversation went on for some time as the counselor instructed me in the many ways I could circumvent the law. In the section above, we talked about "this one part," namely how to avoid getting the baby's father arrested. In the longer section that followed, we talked about "the other part," namely how to dispose of the evidence of the boyfriend's crime, the baby, without getting parental consent. Of course, we didn't use that language. We talked around everything.

I felt bad for the counselor. By participating in abortion and sexual abuse cover-up, she, too, had become a victim of the evil she represented. She didn't want to know the age of my boyfriend or intervene in any way. In her own fashion, it seemed as if she genuinely wanted to help me. Even if that "help" meant killing my baby, skirting Indiana law, and sending me back to my thirty-one-year-old boyfriend without filing the mandated report. By talking in circles long enough, she could block out her role in enabling a crime that virtually all Americans agree is evil—statutory rape.

Although I was only acting the part of a pregnant thirteen-year-old, the problem we documented in the Mona Lisa project was real and widespread. When my friend Phill Kline was elected attorney general of Kansas in 2002, he reviewed the case histories of the 166 abortions performed on girls under fifteen in Kansas during the years 2002 and 2003. Of those 166 cases, the state's abortion clinics reported only three to the state department of Social and Rehabilitation Services. By law, they had to report all 166.[7]

Fully ignoring the reason why Kline challenged the state's Democratic administration to turn over the relevant records, the media turned on Kline with a vengeance. In this solidly red state, Kline lost his 2006 reelection bid to a former Republican whose campaign was fueled by PACs massively funded by the abortion industry, including the nation's leading late-term abortionist, George Tiller. The new attorney general, Paul Morrison, called the outcome "a victory for Kansans who want to make sure their most private personal records are kept private." But Kline never wanted to make those records public. He wanted to use them to prosecute child rape. Like other Kansans, including those in the media, Morrison chose not to acknowledge that by protecting these records he was also indirectly protecting hundreds of child predators.

For its feverish effort to defeat the "anti-choice extremist" Kline, the *Kansas City News* won Planned Parenthood's top editorial honor, the Maggie award, named for its eugenicist founder, Margaret Sanger. Few people wanted to hear the truth, even about child abuse. Kline did not run from the controversy, and he paid a price. There is almost always a price to pay.

Although our videos were released too late to help Kline, they confirmed his data and helped expose Planned Parenthood's casual protection of child predators. In ways no court document could, we showed the willingness of ordinary people to facilitate extraordinary crimes. All of Live Action's work would go on to expose not only the deceptive practices of these abortion facilities, but also the destructive act of abortion itself.

If a picture is worth a thousand words, a video can be worth a million. Today, we all have the tools at our disposal to document and post photos and videos that demonstrate the reality of injustice and evil. It is important not just to tell the story of the victims but to show, graphically if necessary, the brutal devastation of their victimization. We can do our homework, get creative, and find ways to help others *see* and understand the tragedy unfolding around them.

What's at the root of almost every injustice? A lie. A lie about the human person, God, or what justice even means. Most of those who believe the lie simply don't know any better. The dangerous ones are those who do know better. To combat them, we have to study the deception and take the time to understand it. Truth can rehumanize those our opponents have successfully dehumanized. Knowing the truth ourselves is not enough. We have to wield it as a weapon.

CHAPTER 12

Embrace Their Pain

I'll never forget one Planned Parenthood clinic we visited during the Mona Lisa investigation. I was again posing as a thirteen-year-old. As a drop-in, I ended up in one of the clinic's two waiting rooms, the smaller, more cheerful one, if an abortion clinic waiting room can be called that. On the floor was a pile of brightly colored toys.

I wasn't alone. Two women were also sitting there, and they had two beautiful little girls with them, maybe three and five years old, who were playing with the toys. The women looked like sisters. I noticed that one was beginning to show that she was pregnant. She just stared despondently at the ground while the other woman, called "mama" by one of the girls, flipped through a magazine, obviously bored.

Even though I was in character as an underage girl, I wanted to somehow engage the women.

"What are you here for?" I asked the sad-eyed woman. "Abortion?"

"Yes," she said and looked away. She didn't want to talk about it. I felt helpless.

"How about this?" I said, fully off script. "How about we both just leave here? We can go with the people who were outside who said they could help women who were pregnant. Let's just both leave!"

We had passed pro-life sidewalk counselors on the way in. They offered resources and told each woman who came by about a free, confidential pregnancy care center down the street.

The woman looked at me with pain in her eyes and said flatly, "I can't. Please don't talk to me."

Suddenly, the youngest child started jumping up and down, demanding attention and asking her mother for a cup of water. The mother ignored her and continued to flip through her magazine. Then the little girl went over to the woman to whom I'd spoken and pulled on her pant leg.

"Auntie, Auntie!" she said. The child climbed into her aunt's lap and cuddled close to her abdomen. I stared at the little girl, unable to look away. What I saw was the meeting of two cousins, separated by just inches of flesh. I recoiled at the thought that one of these cousins, the unseen one, a little boy or a little girl, would die violently within hours.

Moments later, a Planned Parenthood worker came into the waiting room and called my name. I went in to the second of the two waiting rooms, the inner room that had a lock and a sign on the door that read, without irony, No Children. Behind the locked door were a number of women waiting for their abortions. I was there to do a job, to see how the clinic dealt with sexual abuse, but all I could think of was that sad-eyed woman.

Where were the people to help her? Didn't she know she was not alone? I was proud of the thousands of community pregnancy resource centers that the pro-life movement created. In virtually every community, these pro-bono clinics provided material and financial care to young mothers in need, free of charge, and sometimes offered medical care as well. National organizations also offer ample support, providing counseling, fundraisers, or baby registries for parents in need. Many in the pro-life movement have also welcomed foster children into their homes. Still others provide material support to young parents who struggle. Too many women know none of this. Women and girls need to know that this help exists, and they need encouragement to take advantage of these resources.

Over the years, I've found that many pregnant women considering abortion don't realize how many couples are eager to adopt and have waited years for the opportunity. They don't know they can choose the family who will raise their baby and even maintain a lifelong, loving relationship with their child if they choose.

Women also deserve the facts about the development and humanity of their children and the truth about what an abortion is. Over the years, Live Action has received dozens of messages from women and girls who tell us that it was learning the basic facts about abortion that gave them the clarity to fight for their children's lives.

Planned Parenthood systematically refuses to share this information. Despite its paradoxical position as a source of planned *parenthood* and its delusional claim to be the "leading provider of women's healthcare," Planned Parenthood offers virtually no prenatal care, no material support to young mothers or fathers, and almost certainly no referrals to pregnancy resource centers. Although Planned Parenthood allegedly offers "options counseling," it aborts 160 children for every child it refers for adoption.[1]

Instead of focusing on providing prenatal care or adoption support, abortion facilities profit from the pain of women and kill their children. And they do it in the name of "compassion" and "women's rights." At the same time, abortion advocates accuse the pro-life community of being the ones who fail to support women and children. It is a classic gaslighting tactic, and it should not surprise us. The entire abortion industry depends on lies about human dignity, motherhood, and the pro-life community in order to thrive.

For all my experiences undercover, that afternoon in the waiting room remains one of the most heart-wrenching encounters I've had in an abortion facility. I had seen the sidewalk counselors, eagerly waiting outside and longing to help. I had seen that baby's cousins, beautiful and alive, while he or she waited in the shadow of death. And I witnessed a hopelessness in that young mother that no mother should ever feel.

No matter your cause, it is a gut-wrenching experience to absorb the pain of the victim and a life-changing one to embrace it. Embracing the pain of others leads us to stand up against the ones who are inflicting the pain and to love the ones who are suffering—in this case, mothers and children both. It also means speaking the truth about evil: nothing justifies ending a life, and committing an evil to escape pain only wounds us more. Every woman has the strength inside her to choose life despite the challenges.

For all the thousands who do help mothers and children in need, we need thousands more, millions even. We all share in this ongoing tragedy. We can all share in its resolution. May we embrace the pain of others and make it our own.

CHAPTER 13

Trust God

"Hello, this is Lila Rose. Would you like to donate twenty-five dollars to your alma mater?"

A click at the other end of the line answered my question. I scrolled to the next name and number on my computer screen and dialed again. Another click.

"How's it going for you?" asked my call-center desk mate.

"I'm only getting hung up on about every other time!" I said with a laugh. "How about you?"

"Same. Or they just don't answer," she said.

I pivoted my chair back toward the desk and leaned on it. This sales gig wasn't going so well. Was it really worth the ten dollars an hour I was making?

The answer was no. Walking the mile from my apartment to the UCLA call center and calling alumni all day asking for money didn't seem as important as the investigative reporting I thought was so needed, or the public speaking I was doing. Lives were on the line.

I had already spent both the $1,000 grant from the Leadership Institute and $1,500 of my student loan money to fund printings of *The Advocate*, and the money for the Mona Lisa project had already been spent as well. As much as I needed some income, I quit the call center after a week and went back to activism and school full-time.

The remaining student loan money was only going to last me through the rest of the quarter. I didn't know how I was going to make the additional money I needed, but I felt like I had to take the next right step and focus on my activism.

"God, I entrust my classes and all my finances to you," I prayed. A few days later, in the two-bedroom apartment I shared with four other girls, I received a call from an unknown number. I was in the habit of answering every call I could if I wasn't in class on the chance it was a media call or a useful tip. The call went something like this:

"Hello?"

"Is this Lila Rose?"

"Yes, who's this?"

"My name is Ray Ruddy," he said. "I am a pro-life philanthropist. You were nominated for a Life Prize cash award. You've just won fifty thousand dollars."

I was shocked. I thought for a moment this might be a prank, but Ray did not sound like a prankster.

"Wow. Thank you, Ray. Wow! That's amazing!"

"Don't thank me yet," he said brusquely. "You have to pass the background check first."

I stifled a laugh. Thankfully, I had never been arrested for my pro-life work.

"My staff will be in touch," Ray said.

"Thanks so much again," I stammered, unsure of what to make of the whole thing. After a couple of quick Google searches, I confirmed that Ray was a real philanthropist and that I had actually been selected to receive the prize. I would find out later that Ray, a successful and brilliant businessman, had given away millions to causes—from improving healthcare in developing nations to supporting multiple pro-life organizations—in order to save the lives of vulnerable people.

I was floored. That money could pay for two years of school *and* help fund Live Action. While I was excited to receive it, I was also torn. Why me? Going undercover may have seemed unusual to most people. Focusing so much of my life and work on the pro-life cause surely seemed unusual to many. But I knew how blessed and privileged I was. I had life. I had a loving family and friends. I had the opportunity to attend a great school and advocate for children even while I was a student. All my material needs were met. I knew I was incredibly privileged.

I suspected that Ray was trying to incentivize more people to get involved with the pro-life cause, but I also knew that there were many others out there who were just as deserving, if not more. I thought of all the elderly women and men I had seen, day after day, standing outside abortion facilities praying, regardless of the weather. Some had been keeping vigil for decades, but no one congratulated them, praised them, or gave them cash prizes. The attention they got usually came in the form of angry glares and raised middle fingers.

I knew the prize was a pure gift, one I did not deserve. But I believed that God had a plan and that I should trust him. Over the next few years, I would often reflect on this time in my work. There were times in the future when I didn't know if I would have enough money to pay my staff or fund key programs, times when there were death threats, times when I faced self-doubts that felt overwhelming. I grew especially reflective in those moments when I faced what seemed like impossible obstacles and I wondered what God was doing. Remembering how God had provided for me in the past encouraged me to have faith that God would provide for me in the present.

I also drew hope and inspiration from the stories of others who stepped out in faith and experienced a big breakthrough. One such story was that of Mother Angelica, the now famous nun who founded the largest Catholic media company in the world, Eternal World Television Network (EWTN). Mother Angelica had such faith that God wanted her to start a television station that she made the commitment to purchase a $600,000 satellite even though she did not have the money.

She prayed, trusting that if she was correct in discerning that God wanted her to move forward on the idea, he would provide the means. And he did. The day the satellite arrived (Mother Angelica still didn't have the funds), a man she had never met randomly called her. He had read her writings. He said they transformed his life, and out of gratitude he wanted to make a financial contribution—of $600,000!

When I first started Live Action, I often told God, "Use me, do whatever you want with me. Use me to save lives." I felt an incredible sense of surrender and relief in giving him control. If God were in control, he would figure out the details, right? And God did do incredible and unexpected things! All I had to do was trust him and keep putting one foot in front of the other.

As the years passed, I got wiser about how to build an organization, how to grow a team, how to do media, how to communicate the pro-life message, and how to force political change. As my skills grew, I still felt that deep desire for surrender. I wanted to see God work. I wanted to see something unexpected or incredible happen. I wanted to chalk that something up to "This is God working, not me." I wanted to have confidence in the outcome.

And God does sometimes work that way—but not always. Just as God is at work in the breakthroughs, he is also at work in the struggles. God calls us to love him for his own sake, not just for the prayers he answers. The purest form of love, such as a mother's love for her infant, is the love that expects nothing in return. God wants us to love like that. Trusting God does not guarantee a breakthrough; Jesus promised that following him will bring persecutions, humiliations, and hardships. "You will be hated by all because of my name," he told his disciples. "But the one who endures to the end will be saved" (Matthew 10:22 NRSVCE). Jesus told his followers that they would be "dragged before governors and kings," but he also promised that they wouldn't stand alone—the Holy Spirit would speak through them (Matthew 10:18, 20 NRSVCE). We can be confident that Jesus will never leave us, and he will give us the grace to embrace trials as he did.

If we lose heart when our prayers seem to go unanswered, it's an invitation not to question God's faithfulness but to examine our hearts. Sometimes God moves the mountain for us to demonstrate his power in the form of miracles to help grow our faith. Sometimes, though, God wants us to chip away at the mountain, day in and day out, perhaps for years on end, which means we see only one piece of the work at a time.

I had always thought that if it's meant to be, it will be. God will do it. But then I learned something else. God wants us to learn perseverance. He wants us to use our minds and our talents to seize the opportunities in front of us. He wants us to be faithful, especially when no one is looking and when there is no big breakthrough to encourage us. The angst of decision-making in the midst of uncertainties and the pain that inevitably comes to those who dare to lead are opportunities to mature. He wants us to have grit and to still be thankful, even for the challenges.

Grit is something we can build on. Our sanctification lies in the tension between total trust in God on the one hand and the grinding dedication to an unending task on the other. This tension builds character in a way that no breakthrough can.

In my own dry seasons, I've felt the yearning for consolation more acutely when I hear other people joyfully discuss how God just gave them a breakthrough, and how we would get one ourselves if we only prayed for it. That's my own selfishness. Even when I am stuck in the struggle to overcome my own obstacle, I want to be able to celebrate the breakthroughs of others. What God asks of me, and all of us, is obedience and trust because that is the purest form of love we can give him.

Breakthroughs are never promised on our terms or on our timeline, or even in this life. But that's okay because, as Matthew reminds us, "the one who endures to the end will be saved" (Matthew 24:13 NRSVCE).

CHAPTER 14

Find Your Rock

Rosa Acuna was a young mother of two children. After getting pregnant with her third child, she consulted her doctor about her then six- to eight-week pregnancy and health complications caused by a kidney disorder. According to Rosa, she asked the abortionist "if there was a baby in there," and she said he responded by saying, "Don't be stupid, it's only blood." In court documents, the doctor would say he didn't remember exactly what he told Rosa, but he admitted that it was likely he said that the "seven-week pregnancy is not a living human being," and that her baby was "just tissue at this time."[1]

Her doctor performed the abortion three days later. Back at home, Rosa experienced vaginal bleeding and went to the emergency room. The nurse told her she had the remains of her baby inside her and she would need an operation to extract it from her uterus. That's when Rosa realized her first trimester pregnancy matter was not a blood clot or a bunch of cells. It was a human baby.

Our Live Action team had already established that Planned Parenthood was willing to disregard statutory rape and accept donations offered by a racist donor for the specific purpose of killing Black children. Based on what we'd learned from Rosa's case, we decided to expose another lie that many abortion facilities tell women.

Just as Rosa's doctor had done, we knew that abortionists regularly dehumanized their victims. They had to in order to justify the bloodshed. Planned Parenthood presented itself to the world as a reliable provider of women's health care. So reliable, in fact, that it merited the hundreds of millions of dollars taxpayers poured into its coffers each year.[2]

We wanted to document the lies that Planned Parenthood told women like Rosa in its counseling sessions. Naming the investigation the Rosa Acuna Project, we sent our undercover investigators to clinics in several states. Each investigator claimed to be considering an abortion for herself but wanted accurate medical information first, especially about how developed her preborn baby was.

In Appleton, Wisconsin, clinic staff claimed that a ten-week-old baby in the womb doesn't yet have a heartbeat. In fact, a baby's heart starts beating at about three weeks into pregnancy. In Milwaukee, a clinic staffer insisted that a six-week-old fetus had "no arms, no legs, no heart, no head, no brain."[3] None of that was true. The staffer also lied to make adoption sound more difficult than it is and urged the woman to have an abortion as soon as possible.

In Indianapolis, our investigator, claiming to be ten weeks pregnant, asked the clinic worker when her baby's heart would begin to beat. The worker answered, "It's around . . . I think the eighth or the ninth week that you can hear the heartbeat. . . . It's not a baby, it's a fetus, not like a person."[4] Repeatedly, Planned Parenthood staff would attempt to dehumanize preborn children to encourage would-be clients to have an abortion.

Dealing with all the darkness we were uncovering drove me to a deeper spiritual life. I tried to make time every day to pray, reflect on my experiences in my journal, and read the Bible. In between the travel, the investigations, my classes at UCLA, and the regular media interviews and speeches, I felt torn inside. I had made great friends at UCLA. I was dating, and I loved my dormmates. I didn't feel lonely, but I also felt a desire to grow as a person. I knew that to keep up with my own activism, I had to become stronger. I needed to be more disciplined. I needed to spend more time in prayer. I needed to strengthen my moral compass and character. Every day as I attempted to continue the work, I felt my weaknesses always before me. I knew I needed more help. I wanted to grow in my leadership abilities and, more important, in my spiritual life, and so I began looking for those who could guide me.

During this time, I was also bouncing around from church to church looking for guidance and a community. I already believed that God was real, that he loved me, that I was made in his image. I believed that Christ was God in human flesh, that he had taken on our human nature in order to heal and redeem it so we could participate in eternal life with him. I was a Christian, to be sure, but how was I to really *follow* Christ? What did it mean to become a disciple? How did discipleship integrate with my activism, work, school, friendships, family? And how compatible was my desire to be totally devoted to ending abortion with my desire to also one day be married?

Like many college students, I struggled to find a sustainable rhythm for my life. Although committed to making a difference with my pro-life work, I was not sure how to make the best decisions or how to make the progress I wanted to make. I was juggling the usual stresses of classwork and dating with the unusual stresses of planning and executing national investigations, fundraising, building a nonprofit, and traveling to do media and give speeches on the pro-life cause.

For all the movement in my life, I was starving for direction. I wanted to become the best person I could be, but I did not know how. I did know, however, that if my heart was not rooted in a power greater than myself, in God who was the Way, the Truth, and the Life, I would always struggle to find healing for myself, let alone find the strength I needed to help repair the brokenness in the world around me.

I prayed that the Holy Spirit would guide me to the people who could help me. I started exploring local churches. I checked out a traditional Lutheran church and an evangelical church that met in a movie theater. I also sampled different Christian clubs and Bible study groups on campus.

But as I studied the theology they taught and learned more about the discipleship they offered, I desired more. I weighed their teaching against what the Bible taught through the lens of the wisdom of the early church leaders and some of the greatest thinkers of Christendom over the past two thousand years.

I had grown up reading the church fathers and doctors of the church[5] because my dad included their writings as part of our homeschool curriculum. Thanks to my mother's Latin classes throughout high school (which, next to math, were among my least favorite), I had practice translating articles from Thomas Aquinas's *Summa Theologica* in and out of Latin. I had begun studying Roman Catholicism alongside my dad since the early days of our Catholic bookstore trips but still had many unanswered questions.

Then one Saturday night a girlfriend said to me, "Want to go to Mass with me tomorrow at this women's center near campus?"

Not having any other plans, I said, "Sure."

That Sunday morning, I woke up twenty minutes before the service, pulled on some semi-dressy clothes, and scrambled the half mile or so to an elegant house on a corner in Westwood. I met my friend outside, and we rang the doorbell together. Someone buzzed us in, and we climbed a flight of stairs to a small, light-flooded chapel perched above the home's living room. At the front of the room stood an ornate altar, set against a painting of Jesus and his mother, Mary. The walls of the chapel were set with small stained-glass windows that looked out onto the street.

I was surprised to see only women in the small pews, many of them in their thirties or older, all dressed neatly and professionally. At the time, I knew I had much to learn about Catholic theology and the Mass, but I was impressed by the intentionality and sacredness of it all. I knew enough to know that what Protestants often called *discipleship* or *mentorship*, Catholics called *spiritual direction*. I turned to a woman in the back of the chapel and asked, "Is there anyone here who can give me spiritual direction?"

The woman, whose name was Tessa, asked what spiritual direction meant to me. As she recalls, I answered, "I want to be holy like the Blessed Mother. I want to be holy like Mother Teresa. I want to be holy like my own mother."

"Yes," Tessa said, without skipping a beat. "I can see you this week if you'd like." I was surprised. She answered as though she had expected my question. I found out later that this generous woman, who would become a lifelong friend, had devoted her life to serving and mentoring others. Rather than getting married, Tessa found her vocation in Opus Dei, an institution within the Catholic Church devoted to helping people find God in their daily lives. She had made a pledge to remain celibate and unattached to a family of her own so that she could be wholly devoted to evangelizing and providing spiritual guidance.

At our first meeting, we sat down in a small room next to the house's formal dining room.

"What would you like to get out of our meetings?" Tessa asked.

"I want to become a better woman," I said.

"Got it." She smiled. "Well, what does this better woman look like to you?"

This question led to a long discussion about the women (and men) I admired and why. I told her I wanted to do whatever it took to grow.

"Do you want me to be a straight shooter with you?" Tessa asked.

"Yes," I answered. "You can tell me anything."

"I have some immediate advice," she said, "but you may not like it. Are you sure?"

"Please tell me," I said.

"If you want to grow as a woman, you shouldn't dress like that."

I felt a pang of embarrassment, and I looked down at what I was wearing: flip-flops, cropped yoga pants, and a tank top with my sports bra showing. No, I wasn't going to the gym. I was just going to class and a meeting with Tessa. I realized instantly what Tessa was communicating. Dressing respectfully wasn't just for speaking events; it was for everyone, everywhere.

"You're absolutely right," I said.

I had never taken the time to think about it. It was the first of many areas for improvement that, with Tessa's guidance, I would take time to think about carefully. Thank God for Tessa. Thank God for straight shooters.

Over the next several months, Tessa and I discussed my goals and my habits. We talked about all the responsibilities I was juggling with school and Live Action, as well as my dating and personal relationships. Working together, we made a plan for my personal growth. I wrote down the concrete steps I would take in my day-to-day life to grow as a student, a daughter, an activist, and a Christian. In sum, we strategized how I could be intentional about becoming a better woman.

Tessa and I met once a week. She taught me that the routines and habits of my daily life provided the foundation for my quest to be better. If I neglected to improve those routines, I could not become who I was meant to be. She convinced me that the good I did for my cause was directly linked to the good I did every day. It mattered how I spent the precious time I had been given. One subject we discussed was virtue, a concept that is sadly vanishing in contemporary culture. Tessa said virtue is like a handkerchief: you pick up one corner of it and the rest of it follows. In other words, if I worked on one virtue, the other virtues would be enhanced by the effort. Given that I am a procrastinator by nature and easily distracted, we decided that it would be wisest for me to do the hardest thing on my schedule first each day. With Tessa as my kindly drill sergeant, spiritual boot camp had begun.

As my willpower and self-discipline grew, we added new goals. I reviewed my day every night to see what I had done right and where I had fallen short. I practiced thanking God for all the gifts he had given me. I went to Mass daily. I increased my prayer time to thirty minutes each day. I studied the Catholic Church's teachings more seriously and took theology classes from a wise priest named Father Paul, who also became a spiritual guide and father to me, as well as a source of great wisdom. A year and a half later, I was received into the Catholic Church.

The changes Tessa and Father Paul helped me make may not have been obvious to the rest of the world, but I sensed the change within. I was working on my inner virtue, the quiet things I did every day that nobody else may have noticed. Inner virtue is not flashy, and even the smallest changes take hard work. To paraphrase legendary UCLA basketball coach John Wooden, "The true test of character is what someone does when no one is watching." No matter how impressive or important our external contributions to the world, none of it matters if our souls are not right before God. And mentors can help guide us there.

Mentors get to know us personally so they can speak directly into our lives. A mentor gets in the ring with us and teaches us how to fight. We can learn a tremendous amount from the examples of our heroes and through interactions with our friends and community, but a mentor goes deeper. At our request, a mentor challenges us, guides our progress, and holds us accountable. A mentor not only helps us monitor our progress but also encourages and inspires us when our progress lags.

We cannot expect a mentor to just show up. We have to ask for mentorship. We have to seek it out. We have to explain why we need help and open ourselves to the help a good mentor can provide. We also need to be prepared to study and learn.

While they are a tremendous source of wisdom, mentors aren't there to answer all our life questions. Making decisions for us is not part of their job description. They don't instruct us on what to fight for. They don't tell us which job to take, which person to date, or whom to marry, but they do help us discern what God is guiding us to do. They help us grow in knowledge, virtue, and prayer so we can better follow where Christ is leading us. To ground ourselves for our mission, we have to find our rock, the anchor for our faith. A good mentor can lead us there.

CHAPTER 15

Be Teachable

I asked for help from Tessa for my personal development, and I was blessed to receive Father Paul's guidance for my spiritual growth, but I knew I needed coaches for my professional development as well. We stop growing if we think we have little left to learn. A core part of any team is the coach. Athletes only make it to the Olympics with a good coach. They need someone to push them, train them, and help them be better. We all need coaches.

I would have never been able to build Live Action were it not for the coaches I sought out, good men and women who generously helped me along the way. I saw the importance of accepting coaching early on when a friend helped me get Live Action's first website up and running. I was still in college at the time, but I was routinely doing media interviews about our investigative journalism, and we sometimes saw a spike in website traffic after an appearance. My friend had been careful to include a support button on our website, and it was usually after a new investigative release that we'd get some unexpected donations.

One afternoon I got back to my apartment after class and saw that someone had donated one thousand dollars online. I immediately did a Google search and discovered that he was the CEO and founder of his own company. I was acquainted with only a handful of business leaders and entrepreneurs at the time and was eager to find advisors to help guide Live Action's growing platform. I wanted to thank this new donor, but I also thought he might be able to help us with more than a financial contribution. A little nervous, I picked up the phone and dialed his number.

A receptionist picked up. "Hello, how can I help you?"

"Hi, my name is Lila Rose with the group Live Action." I asked if the donor was available to talk.

"Can you hold please?"

I had prepared what I wanted to say by googling "how to talk to a donor" and finding a helpful resource. The basic message went something like this: Thank donors profusely. Find out what they are passionate about. Find out why they donated. Get to know them. Ask if you can share with them the impact of their dollars. Ask how you can best stay in touch.

The donor and I talked for ten minutes, and he expressed surprise that I had called him. "Most of the time when I donate, I don't hear from the organization for months," he said. "I donated today, and the president of the organization calls me!"

I may be the president, I thought, *but I'm also the only staff!* I kept that little detail to myself. I learned that our donor was a driven and brilliant self-starter who had built his company from scratch and was deeply passionate about causes that defended the most vulnerable. When I asked if he would give me business advice, he said he would—and he did, generously.

As a high-achieving CEO, he taught me the importance of self-care as a leader. Managing the responsibilities of a company (or in my case, a nonprofit) and the huge mission of Live Action can be never-ending and all-consuming. My donor encouraged me to take time each day to sweat—to exercise intensely so that I could keep up with the mental and emotional intensity of my job. We also had long talks about my relationships with my staff. As a boss, I had to be careful with my words and my behavior. What I said and did carried extra weight because of my position of authority and could be easily misunderstood. It was a long distance from my early days of activism where I partnered with peers, not employees.

Eventually, the donor would also pay for a corporate coach to do a series of life-changing sessions with me and another team member. He has remained a friend and mentor to this day.

Some years later, a friend introduced me to another entrepreneur with a huge heart for the pro-life cause who also agreed to coach me. Each week by phone we discussed the challenges I faced personally as a leader and the challenges Live Action faced as an organization. He gave me the framework to think about strategic planning and the creation of monthly, yearly, and multiyear plans for our organization. Every week we reviewed my personal progress toward those goals, as well as the progress of my team. Thanks to his incredibly helpful guidance, I was able to anticipate and solve problems I would not have been able to solve on my own.

Sometimes you need a coach to give you the organizational equivalent of a half-time talk. I was reminded of this when prepping footage for release of one of our national investigations. A PR firm for which we had broken our budget was helping with statements, op-eds, media relations, and interview booking. I had asked the firm to assign its best writer to our case and was assured we would get the best of everything.

It did not work out that way. The press release I got back sounded boring to me. *How had someone on the firm's team managed to make such a bombshell investigation sound boring? What am I paying them for, anyway?* I asked myself and hurried off to an interview.

After a few meetings and Mass, I got back to my computer feeling frustrated. The PR firm was not giving me or this project serious attention. We were in the middle of a major media campaign exposing Planned Parenthood, and we needed to do better getting our message out. I knew I couldn't be a one-woman editorial board. I called up a mentor of mine and complained to him.

"They aren't taking me seriously!" I said. "If I weren't a twenty-one-year-old woman, I feel like they would do a better job with the stuff they are sending me."

"You need to tell them what you think and ask for them to do better," my mentor said.

"I have done that," I said, exasperated. "I told them to assign their best people."

"Well, you have to call him and talk to him, man to man. Forget that you're a woman and you're only twenty-one. You are paying them top dollar, and this is really important. Don't let anyone look down on you because you're young."

"Okay," I said. I hated the idea of having conflict with one of our vendors, especially at such a crucial time. How would he respond?

"Can I practice saying to you what I'll say to him?" I asked my mentor.

"Of course, go for it."

We went through the scenario a few times together, and then I e-mailed the account lead.

Hey, Sam, can you chat for a few minutes?

He was quick to respond, and we jumped on the phone.

"Sam," I said as calmly as I could, given how nervous I felt about being so direct. "The last op-ed was simply not acceptable. I need you to find a better writer."

This was a demand, not a request. Sam heard the difference in my voice. Suddenly his tone shifted.

"You got it, Lila, okay. Enzo will do the writing."

Enzo was one of their senior leaders, and I knew personally he was a great writer.

"Thanks, Sam," I said. "I really appreciate it."

They got the message. From then on, the writing was markedly better. I got my coach's message too. "Now, go out there, Lila, and win that game." To stand up for life meant standing up for smaller, more tangible objectives along the way. We have to demand better from ourselves and, sometimes, from the people we work with. A good coach can remind us.

This is rarely easy. Holding others accountable makes most of us uncomfortable, especially if we don't like conflict. If the cause is important, then mediocre cannot become the norm. When the best is demanded, we cannot talk ourselves out of conflict by seeking refuge in our age or sex or any other *seeming* limitation. Nor can we expect our coaches to do our work for us. To stand up is to grow up and demand better.

Any number of professional people are qualified to teach and guide us. Many of them are more than willing to serve as a coach, especially if they believe in our cause. Chances are that they are often asked for money or jobs or other favors. Rarely are they asked for their wisdom.

Another invaluable mentor of mine is organizational guru Pat Lencioni. I met Pat through Joanna, one of Live Action's team members and brave investigative reporters. Having learned to seek out the best mentors she could find, Joanna called Pat out of the blue. As part of Live Action's training, Joanna had read some of his books. After checking out his bio, Joanna noticed they had a connection—both she and Pat had graduated from Claremont McKenna College.

Sensing an opportunity, Joanna sent an e-mail explaining her work for a nonprofit and noting their shared alma mater. Upon reading it, Pat decided to make time for a call. When he discovered we did pro-life work, he excitedly shared that it was a passion of his, too, and he volunteered to help us in any way he could. Thanks to Joanna's smart initiative, Pat became a mentor for us and generously donated whole days of his valuable time to help our team.

Finding the right people to ask for advice may take some trial and error. Over the years, not everyone I have asked is available to give me advice, and even fewer are available to do regular coaching. But ultimately, finding coaches doesn't need to be complicated. It mainly requires a willingness to keep asking for advice from people we admire and respect, and then a commitment to show up regularly when someone agrees to help.

Ask yourself: *Who do I know who is more experienced than me, who also cares about my cause? Who is someone I admire both personally and professionally?* Maybe it is someone you've met through your faith community, through friends or family, or through community service activities. Perhaps it's someone who financially supports good causes, or someone who already volunteers.

It can be easy to get excited about finding the right person, one you can call and with whom you can occasionally meet, but maintaining this communication requires commitment from both of you. A coach has to take his or her role seriously. That requires a commitment of time and patience.

We, the "coachees," need a teachable and humble spirit. We must prioritize the time with our coaches and do the homework they suggest. Consistency is critical. So is honesty about our weaknesses. While it may not come easily, we need to be open and candid about our struggles. As humble students, we must be willing to acknowledge the truth about ourselves, the good and the bad, and all we have left to learn. As we grow, our pursuit of the truth should only intensify. No matter our age, a teachable spirit is key to growth.

CHAPTER 16

Focus

In the years I spent documenting sexual abuse cover-ups at abortion facilities, I had come across a troubling pattern: victims of sexual abuse were sometimes also victims of human trafficking. Government agencies estimated that there were hundreds of thousands of sex-trafficked children. I knew that these victims often became pregnant. I wanted to know what happened to these girls when they did.

As much as I was willing to go undercover myself, I was becoming recognizable, regardless of my hair color, which made it imperative that I change my role from player to coach. For months, I worked to recruit and train a new team of investigative reporters for this new project. In 2011, Live Action initiated another multistate trip to investigate the willingness of Planned Parenthood facilities to aid and abet sex traffickers of young girls. I had focused most of my research on Planned Parenthood because it was the largest abortion chain in the nation, committing at the time one-fourth of all abortions, and now more than a third.[1]

Following a carefully planned itinerary, our small team headed to New Jersey. The Garden State in January is no joke. We pulled our Jeep to the side of the road, and I opened the passenger door to hop out. As I tried to push the door open, it jammed against a pile of icy snow, preventing me from opening it all the way. We were in a hurry and so I had to squeeze out as best as I could. The crunch of the heavily packed snow beneath my boots reminded me of how much I missed California. I traded seats with Raul in the back seat to help Giovanna get her camera placed.

"How are you feeling, G?" I asked.

"Good! I feel good," she said.

She and Raul were total champs. They were preparing to go undercover into a Planned Parenthood abortion clinic down the street. We were going to run a scenario in which Raul played a pimp and Giovanna played his assistant. In the scenario, they were running an illicit sex ring of fourteen- and fifteen-year-old girls. They had been prepping for weeks and had already gone to other abortion clinics in the days prior. I waited in the car impatiently with David Daleiden, already a Live Action veteran of several years, and watched the snow fall softly on the pavement around us.

Across the street from the abortion clinic was a cemetery. The small tombstones jutted up against the growing blanket of ice and snow. In the back section of the abortion clinic, smoke rose from the building. We wondered aloud what it could be.

"Probably a crematorium," David said grimly.

We had done our research. We knew cremation was one of the ways abortion clinics disposed of the bodies of their victims. The children killed here by an abortionist were placed into an oven to be incinerated, their small bodies turning into smoke, like the smoke we saw rising into the cold sky. There was no one to mourn them, to bury them, to remember them, to visit their graves.

The minutes passed as we sat in silence feeling the weight of the horror and tragedy across the street. Suddenly, there was a tap on the window. It was Raul. His face looked pained and tense. He and Giovanna were back early from the clinic. We unlocked the door, and they both jumped into the back seat.

"What happened?" I asked anxiously as David pulled out into the street. "How did it go?"

"It was so busy in there," Giovanna said quietly. "So many women, all sitting in there. Some of them looked really pregnant, like *really* pregnant. The staff were too busy to see us."

As we drove away, we exchanged helpless looks. Every single baby was scheduled to die that day in that facility. We hadn't saved anyone. Each little boy and girl in that room was facing death alone with no one to advocate for them.

I felt the familiar sting of helplessness. It was much the same sting I felt the first time I stood outside an abortion clinic to pray and the first time I went into a clinic undercover. I contemplated again how women were being told abortion was empowering for them and that millions continued to accept the false "choice" of abortion. My mind struggled to process the weight of the bloodshed and suffering. I was leading my team, we had a job to do, and there wasn't much time to process the human destruction we were witnessing. As I had done on other investigative trips, I allowed myself to ignore the painful emotions welling up deep in my heart until I had a chance later, when our work was done for the day, to let myself weep.

When we arrived at the next clinic in Perth Amboy, New Jersey, Raul and Giovanna headed in. The conversation they recorded with the manager of that clinic would shock even pro-abortion advocates. My two teammates explained that they managed a sex ring of underage girls in the country and needed access to cheap, confidential birth control and abortions. The Planned Parenthood office manager, Amy Woodruff, proved eager to help them.

Woodruff told them not to report the girls' ages as that triggered reporting requirements. "For the most part, we want as little information as possible," Woodruff said. When asked if the girls could obtain abortions, Woodruff recommended that the pimp and his associate go to another clinic whose "protocols are not as strict as ours."[2] When Woodruff helpfully explained that the girls could not have intercourse for a minimum of two weeks after having an abortion, Raul rose to the moment.

In the role of a disgruntled pimp, he asked how the girls would be able to "make money" during those off weeks.

Woodruff didn't hesitate. She recommended that Raul use the girls' bodies "waist up."[3] She spoke as matter-of-factly as if she were telling him how to arrange the merchandise in a display window. Marketing advice. Her attitude and words were devoid of any empathy or conscience. Watching the video of the day's investigation in the hotel room that night, I felt a sense of numbness. It was hard to process how truly banal the evil was, how normal and carelessly Woodruff talked. She behaved like this was normal behavior for her and normal treatment for the girls and women who walked through her door. The cruel dehumanization of children not yet born was also extended to their mothers.

Woodruff was hardly unique. In Richmond, Virginia, a Planned Parenthood staffer told our investigator posing as a sex trafficker how to get around parental consent laws to obtain abortions for the trafficked minor girls. In Washington, DC, our nation's capital, a staffer counseled the trafficker on how to get the girls tested for STIs, how to work the system without health insurance, and how best to secure the girls an abortion. In Roanoke, Virginia, a staffer told our trafficker, "From the age of twelve up, for birth control, you can just come in and do that. You don't have to have a parent, okay?" In the Bronx, when our trafficker explained that the girls he managed were as young as fourteen, the staffer reassured him, "We see people as young as thirteen. . . . Everything is totally confidential."

Everywhere our team went that winter, the pattern was the same. Turning a blind eye to the sex trafficking of underage immigrant girls, Planned Parenthood staffers promoted abortion with the fervor of used car salesmen from hell.

As we edited the videos and designed a release strategy, we firmed up our plans to go to more Planned Parenthood clinics to get even more footage. However, that plan wasn't to be. In January 2011, the day before the annual March for Life in Washington, I got a phone call from a Reuters reporter. I thought he was going to ask me about the March for Life, but instead, the reporter asked me flat out, "Is it true that people from your group are posing as sex traffickers?" I took a deep breath, my mind racing. How did he know to ask that? Someone at Planned Parenthood must have figured out our strategy and tipped him off.

"The footage will speak for itself," I responded as calmly as I could. My mind was racing. Planned Parenthood was trying to spike our story by giving it to the press before we did. I knew we had to break the story before Planned Parenthood had a chance to control the narrative with its own preemptive report. I called the investigations to a halt. Planned Parenthood would obviously put its employees on alert. They might even comply with the law for a few weeks, or at least pretend to. This left us no choice but to start releasing the video we had shot.

I was already in Washington, DC, for the March for Life and decided to stay in town for another week. This was an opportunity to try to defund Planned Parenthood of the hundreds of millions of dollars a year they received in taxpayer funds. My only other staffer at the time, Dani, agreed to spend the week with me. We were living out of a hotel while I did media interviews and met with members of Congress and other heads of pro-life groups.

It was a crazy time.

The battle to keep my eyes fixed on the goal was highlighted in one interview I did during that time. I had been up the whole night before editing our next video for release and had spent the morning, beginning at six o'clock, doing back-to-back media appearances and meetings. In the afternoon, I hopped in a taxi and headed bleary-eyed to CNN's Washington studio for a remote interview with one of its on-air hosts, Brooke Baldwin. After arriving, I sat in the makeup chair trying to concentrate on what I would say in the interview. As I looked in the mirror, I thought, *CNN makeup is no Fox News makeup.* It didn't matter. No amount of makeup could cover the dark circles under my eyes.

"Lila Rose?" A camera technician leaned his head into the greenroom. "You're on."

I followed him down the hallway and into a small studio, where he miked me for the remote. I breathed a prayer, hoping I wouldn't fall asleep in the chair or say something incoherent. Through my earpiece, I heard a voice say, "Program starting in fifteen seconds!"

The program opened, and Brooke began asking a series of tough questions.[4] The one that I would remember was this: "Do you, Lila, have this myopic agenda to take down this federally funded group, and do you think you'll be successful?"

"First of all, Brooke, you can read our mission," I responded. "We state it clearly on our website. Our goal is to expose the abuse cover-up, the corruption, the illicit activity going on every day in abortion clinics."

Once the interview was over, I had to laugh. Our narrative was powerful enough and our evidence strong enough that it seemed to deprive the reporter of reasonable objection. Would she have asked those same hostile questions to an environmental activist, a gun control activist, or even a pro-abortion activist? I doubt it. If Brooke knew that there were centers in her city legally killing one-year-olds, would she use the word *myopic* to describe efforts to stop the killing? I hope not.

In a similar vein, if Brooke knew that a corporation was willing to help sex traffickers succeed in their business, would she call the efforts of those trying to stop the traffickers myopic? Of course not. What made our efforts myopic in her view was our target.

Intentionally or not, Brooke had confused myopia with focus. Myopia, as Brooke used it, is a narrow view or a lack of discernment. Focus, however, is intentional concentration and effort. Of course, I was focused and determined. Without focus, I would not be sitting in a CNN studio talking to Brooke Baldwin. Without focus, I would be back in California, hanging out with my peers, wondering how the surf was running at Santa Cruz, not wrestling to replace CNN's false narrative with the truth.

If anyone was myopic, it was most media groups, not us. Virtually all major newspaper editorial boards support abortion. Most major media groups support abortion. Their myopic support for abortion has devastating effects on their reporting.

For example, for sixteen years Pennsylvania health authorities and the Philadelphia media had turned a blind eye to the practice of an abortionist named Kermit Gosnell. In fact, had law enforcement not searched his premises in a prescription opioid raid, Gosnell might never have been brought to justice.

Most of what Gosnell did every day was legal. He killed children up through nine months of pregnancy, operating in squalid conditions on mostly low-income and minority women. Some of the women died due to the unsanitary conditions and his unsafe procedures. In the case of failed abortions, and there were several, he simply cut the spines of babies alive outside the womb and killed them. In May 2013, Gosnell was convicted of three counts of first-degree murder and one count of involuntary manslaughter in the death of a patient.

The media paid little attention to the case, and when they were finally embarrassed into covering Gosnell's trial—a blogger posted a picture of an empty press section in the courtroom that went viral—they accepted the spin of activists such as Ilyse Hogue, president of NARAL Pro-Choice America. "Justice was served to Kermit Gosnell today and he will pay the price for the atrocities he committed," Hogue told the *New York Times*, confident the reporter would parrot her talking point. "Anti-choice politicians, and their unrelenting efforts to deny women access to safe and legal abortion care, will only drive more women to back-alley butchers like Kermit Gosnell."[5] It didn't matter that this wasn't the "back-alley"— most of the atrocities Gosnell had committed were perfectly legal.

Despite the bias of most media groups, our sex-trafficking videos were shocking enough and were viewed often enough through social media that even the *New York Times* felt compelled to respond. Staying on message, Stuart Schear, vice president for communications of Planned Parenthood, told the *Times* that Planned Parenthood had "zero tolerance" for unethical behavior and that the behavior filmed at the Perth Amboy clinic was "very isolated."[6] Planned Parenthood also called me an "anti-choice extremist" who was trying to "discredit" the organization through "selectively edited" footage, fully ignoring the fact that we released the unedited footage to any media group that requested it.

Having seen firsthand numerous instances of unethical behavior by Schear's colleagues over the previous four years, I could have assured him there was nothing "isolated" about this incident. In an effort to prove its lies, Planned Parenthood made Woodruff, the Perth Amboy Manager, their scapegoat and fired her. She made the mistake of getting caught.

But our evidence was stronger than their denials. The videos forced their way into network coverage. For a week, almost every primetime cable and network news show covered the investigations with, of course, an inevitable spin. ABC, for instance, interviewed me for thirty minutes, asking me the same questions over and over again but included only Planned Parenthood's defense in their piece. The producers were content to stick an image of me being interviewed in the background.

A week after the first video's release, we knew we needed more time on the ground in Washington, DC. I negotiated with the hotel manager for a larger room at a fixed rate for the next two weeks. Thankfully, the beautiful and historic St. Matthew's Cathedral was two blocks down the street, and I was able to stop there every day to attend Mass and pray in the middle of the storm. With Father Paul's and Tessa's encouragement, I made that prayer my daily priority. It was prayer that helped me focus—and remembering that God, who was all-powerful and all-loving, would win the ultimate war for justice.

The forces that can shake our focus are usually not the ones typical to the battle. During those weeks, I faced attacks from the abortion industry and their supporters: personal negative news reports, online trolls mocking me, and even multiple death and rape threats. There was even a fake site that imposed my face on pornographic images. But these attacks were to be expected, and they showed me that I was over the target. Instead of derailing my focus, all these things reminded me this was a life-and-death battle and there was a cost.

What troubled me more than death threats was hearing some leaders of likeminded organizations say behind closed doors that they couldn't support our efforts because the "time wasn't right yet," leaders who didn't seem to think that defunding the abortion industry was even *possible*, at least not for years or even decades. These should have been our allies; instead, they were becoming obstacles. They had other agendas, and defunding Planned Parenthood wasn't one of them. It seemed to me that for some of them the time would never be right.

What threatened my focus the most during those weeks had nothing to do with our investigation or the attacks or obstacles we faced. It had to do with an ex-boyfriend. He had pursued me for years. We had become close friends, and then we started dating. Our relationship had begun to bring into focus some of my own wounds from childhood, which I hadn't yet come to understand and process. I also didn't have good boundaries or the experience needed to recognize unhealthy patterns in a relationship, and there were plenty of these patterns in ours. Despite the good advice of friends and family, I struggled to maintain boundaries with him once we broke up. We had just broken up a month before, and it didn't help that he lived in DC and showed up to the churches where I prayed or events I attended. And now he was leaving me letters at the front desk of the hotel, pleading to get back together.

If I ever thought I was some sort of superwoman, that week sent me crashing back to earth. While all the activity of the media and political battle was demanding my attention and energy, the heartache I felt over my ex and the unexpressed grief over the childhood wounds that our relationship had unearthed felt destabilizing. Years later, I would learn to recognize and grieve the impact of the specific challenges and hurts in my own childhood, the stress I had internalized from my mother and the struggles in my parents' marriage. But for now, it all felt like a swirling vortex deep beneath the surface that sometimes threatened to pull me under.

One night, desperately needing a few hours of sleep before an early morning interview, I lay in bed crying. I didn't even have the words to express why I felt the pain I was feeling. I only knew to pray, "God, help me, I need you." Although full clarity and healing didn't come that night, or even for years, God gave me the peace and strength to persevere. In those quiet, painful moments that no one sees—and we all have them—there is no one better to surrender to.

Despite the internal struggles and the external chaos, those weeks of laserlike focus in Washington, DC, were making a historic impact.

Our video evidence was powerful enough to incite Congress to act in an unprecedented way. The House of Representatives voted for the first time in history to defund Planned Parenthood of their half a billion a year in taxpayer dollars. The vote was bipartisan; several Democrats and Independents joined Republicans. This was an extraordinary move, the first and only time it ever happened, and our "myopic" efforts had made it possible.

Our next obstacle was the Senate, then controlled by Democrats. Surely, we thought, even rock-solid abortion defenders couldn't defend or ignore the abuses we'd documented. They'd at least investigate them. Politically, both sides would have no choice but to take action and stop the government funding. Or so I hoped. Unfortunately, pro-choice senators were not about to buck the abortion industry that helped fund their campaigns, and then-President Barack Obama gave no indication they ought to. He met regularly with the head of Planned Parenthood, with whom he had a close relationship, and that was all the signal the Senate needed.

Looking back on this particular battle, I have to marvel, not at our ultimate failure to defund Planned Parenthood at the time, but at our ability to get so close. The vote by the House of Representatives proved that defunding Planned Parenthood was a viable political goal. It had never been done before. I was twenty-two at the time. My teammates were no older. We took on a billion-dollar corporation and its powerful allies and ignited momentum to bring them down.

We did this because we had stayed the course with our investigative work over a period of years. We had begun with exposing sexual abuse cover-up in Los Angeles clinics, then exposed that abuse cover-up nationally, and then expanded the investigation to the aiding and abetting of traffickers.

If we had stopped our investigative work after our first few tries, we would never have made it this far. The reality is, we'll make little progress if we are constantly giving up on one project or strategy to start a new one. A good project, completed, has more value and impact than a dozen projects we never finish. We have to keep our focus.

As you and I fight for our causes, both the opportunities and challenges we face can make it increasingly difficult to keep that focus. We may see hundreds of opportunities, as well as reasons why we should try something and then reasons why we shouldn't. For every person cheering us on, there may be a hundred critics. And the personal struggles we face may be even more daunting.

Along the way, we may also be ridiculed for our focus. This is inevitable. Maybe we will face negative attention from peers or even from the media. Maybe there will be a comment online, perhaps from a friend, that will feel like a knife in the back or a slap in the face. This is all part of the battle, and many who oppose us may treat us poorly.

How do we keep our focus? Ultimately, we remember for whom and for what we are fighting: the principle that needs defending, the injustice that needs exposing, the vulnerable person who cries out for help. In the tough moments, we can lean on our mentors and friends, take time to rest and pray, and then return to the battle. There is no turning back or backing down. The more we focus and the more doggedly we strive for our goal, the less likely it is that we will be stunned by the darts that inevitably come from all sides.

CHAPTER 17

Expect Resistance from Within

When I first started doing investigative journalism, not everyone who was pro-life agreed with my strategy. Journalists, of course, have been doing undercover work for more than a century. In 1887, Nellie Bly, a twenty-three-year-old journalist, feigned insanity to get admitted to a mental institution. She courageously spent ten days as a patient to document the institution's abuse of patients. When Joseph Pulitzer published Bly's exposé in the *New York World*, she was treated as a hero, and reformers took up her cause.

Government authorities, such as police and military, have been doing undercover work for centuries. Infiltrating one's opponent is a part of any war. Nevertheless, some pro-life leaders, Catholics in particular, used the media interest around my work as an opportunity to criticize our tactics as unethical. They felt that going undercover was immoral because it involved deception.

Such resistance from within my own ranks should not have surprised me. Throughout history, some good souls within every social movement have urged their activist allies to slow down, and they typically do so by criticizing not their cause but their tactics.

During his fight for civil rights, Martin Luther King Jr. was frequently accused of being too controversial and criticized for his tactics. King specifically designed protests that would garner attention. His goal was to shine a light on the indignities Blacks suffered under Jim Crow by forcing it into the forefront of the nation's field of vision. He understood that television—by the 1950s nearly every household had a TV—gave his movement the visibility it needed but had never had. It was one thing to read about police reacting to his demonstrations with brute force. It was another thing to see it in action. It always pays to understand the media.

King was just twenty-six years old when, in 1955, he first gained national attention leading the Montgomery bus boycott. In 1963, he ignored an unjust judicial restriction on his First Amendment rights to speech and assembly by leading a series of speeches and sit-ins in Birmingham, Alabama. He was promptly arrested and imprisoned.

Also in 1963, local ministers and religious leaders, many of whom agreed with King's platform, nevertheless admonished him publicly for what they considered extremist tactics. Eight Alabama clergymen wrote King a public letter, criticizing his "extreme measures" and accusing his actions of inciting "hatred and violence."[1] In his famous "Letter from a Birmingham Jail," King addressed Christian detractors, specifically the "white moderates," whose "lukewarm acceptance" King found "more bewildering than outright rejection."

> While confined here in the Birmingham city jail, I came across your recent statement calling my present activities "unwise and untimely." . . . Actually, we who engage in nonviolent direct action are not the creators of tension. We merely bring to the surface the hidden tension that is already alive. We bring it out in the open, where it can be seen and dealt with. Like a boil that can never be cured so long as it is covered up but must be opened with all its ugliness to the natural medicines of air and light, injustice must be exposed, with all the tension its exposure creates, to the light of human conscience and the air of national opinion before it can be cured.[2]

The atrocities taking place in abortion facilities must also be brought out in the open, and the injustice "exposed, with all the tension its exposure creates."

Conflict from within our own community is painful, especially when directed at us. As human beings, we are predisposed to want harmony. Peer pressure is a natural phenomenon that helps individuals within a society know what behavior is and isn't considered appropriate. Ultimately, however, we must care more about our cause than the opinions of those around us, both friend and foe. We have to be willing to have hard conversations about an injustice, to demand better, and even to take peaceful but forceful action to make society better, even at the cost of our own standing in the community, and possibly even at the risk of our own freedom and safety.

The criticism Live Action received because we did undercover work felt unfair to me. There had to be Christians in the police force, in government agencies, and in media who had been involved in undercover work long before I ever set foot in an abortion clinic. The FBI's most celebrated undercover agent, Joe "Donnie Brasco" Pistone, was a Catholic who "still went to mass when [he] could sneak away from the crew."[3] And yet, I had never even heard of a public debate about whether or not it was acceptable for Christians in law enforcement to assume undercover roles to investigate criminals and hold them accountable for their crimes.

Civil authorities had abdicated their responsibility to investigate and close abortion facilities. The government, whose job it is to protect the most vulnerable against those who would exploit and destroy them, was expressly *permitting* the violence. This is why Live Action's investigative work began—because of a failure of the law and law enforcement to protect children in the womb and their mothers from the abortion industry.

Undercover reporting was a last resort but a necessary one. It was not possible to simply call Planned Parenthood's public relations team and expect an honest answer about whether or not they covered up sexual abuse, enabled sex traffickers, or did gender-specific abortions. Of course, they would deny any such accusations. Yet, I knew that these abuses were routine and widespread and needed to be exposed. I knew, too, that by exposing them, we would have the opportunity to speak against the ultimate horror in those facilities: the killing of preborn children.

Sometimes resistance from within can come not only from our allies but from those who are supposed to be neutral parties. As we continued to release our investigative campaigns year after year, our online following grew rapidly, with millions of people beginning to view and share our content monthly. But we soon discovered that we faced resistance as well from entities that were supposed to be neutral partners in our effort to publish our work: namely the large social media platforms.

When several major social media companies took note of how effectively we were using their platforms, they violated their own terms of service to block us. Twitter banned both my account and Live Action's account from all advertising. To continue advertising, we were told we would have to delete ultrasound images, our undercover investigations, all references to abortion, and all criticism of Planned Parenthood—not only from our Twitter feeds but also on our website. In contrast, Planned Parenthood was permitted to continue advertising, spending hundreds of thousands of dollars a year promoting pro-choice tweets. Other pro-abortion activist groups, such as ReproAction, could also run ads, including an ad calling for pro-life groups to be banned from Twitter.

Pinterest was even worse. An insider revealed that its employees had purposefully added Live Action to a "porn block list" to prevent our content from being shared on the platform. After we made this public, Live Action's account was permanently suspended. We fought the suspension by appealing it and widely publicizing what had happened. Later, Facebook would allow abortionists to fact check our pages through a third-party fact-checking service and assign strikes to our accounts. The strikes threatened to restrict our ability to reach our own followers. After we proved the abortionists' fact checking was unfair and incorrect, Facebook removed the strikes but allowed the abortionists to continue to serve as fact checkers.

What do we do when we face opposition, whether from our own allies or supposedly neutral parties? In the words of Jesus, "Blessed are you when people revile you and persecute you and utter all kinds of evil against you falsely on my account" (Matthew 5:11 NRSVCE). Jesus warned and consoled his followers that persecution would come. Even so, that doesn't make it easier to absorb, especially when it comes from our allies.

Don't be scandalized when resistance from those closest to you may come. Use it as an opportunity to either reaffirm your approach or to evaluate if there is a way you can improve. Long before some Christians accused me of sinning by doing undercover work, I had thought through and prayed about the decision to go undercover and taken stock of my own intentions.

The good news is that resistance from within will always have an upside: if the critics are right, they may help us recognize blind spots we have, or, if they are wrong, they will give us an opportunity to build resilience and determination to forge ahead.

The key is never to use criticism—from either our allies or our opponents—as an excuse to give up instead of to grow. We should examine our consciences, check our intentions, and continue the fight. True character is forged in the hard work of perseverance as we fight to serve others, especially when those close to us may stand in our way.

CHAPTER 18

Keep the Pressure On

We had made a major dent with our sex-trafficking videos, but we had to make more than a dent. I knew that it was essential to build enough political will so that when the pro-life side had more seats in the Senate and occupied the White House, there would be a robust movement to get the job done and defund the abortion corporation.

I also knew we could do much more. My goal was nothing short of enacting legal protection for the child in the womb and to do so within five years. But how could we achieve legal protection for preborn children when Planned Parenthood was receiving billions in taxpayer dollars and in turn spending millions to protect abortion's legality? As much as I knew I would miss California, I felt that I had to stay long-term in DC to keep the pressure on and grow the movement. Keeping the pressure on would require inner perseverance to the daily work in front of me. It also meant that we must relentlessly expose the evil we were battling.

Every year, Live Action continued to launch major investigations on serious issues, creating media campaigns that reached millions and called for the defunding of the abortion industry. We decided that if we continued to expose abortion facilities, and did so year after year with explosive investigative reports, surely we could build the political momentum necessary to at least defund Planned Parenthood of its taxpayer dollars. With that goal accomplished, we could leverage the momentum to work toward total legal protection for children in the womb.

I set up an office in Washington and worked hard to recruit a team that could handle the various aspects of our work—fundraising, video production, news writing, grassroots activation, and social media. There was so much trial and error. In the beginning, I could afford to hire only entry-level staff, and while I met and worked with some very dedicated and smart people, I also made mistakes. It was a hard lesson to learn that people I hired who were zealous advocates of a cause did not always make reliable, day-to-day workers. I was learning on the job in a political environment that had little tolerance for error.

Those first years in DC taught me the stark realities of politics and organization building. We faced a decades-old entrenchment of apathy and inaction around abortion. Yes, we were featured regularly on con-servative TV shows. We riled up activists and fired up a few Republican members of Congress. I met with Senate leaders. They listened politely and agreed with me in principle. Some even spoke with me at press con-ferences or rallies. However, we also faced many obstacles. Perhaps the biggest obstacle of all was the desperate fear many political leaders had of an openly hostile media, and how the media's negative coverage of their words or votes might impact their reputation with constituents.

At one private meeting of about fifty politicians and staffers, I was invited to present my findings about Planned Parenthood. Other activists also spoke to the group about their issues. Then there was a session for activists and NGO leaders to ask questions of members of Congress. The chief of staff for the House majority leader was present and was asked point blank why they weren't playing hardball with the Senate over the budget that would be sent to then-President Obama.

The House had the power to remove from the budget funding for Planned Parenthood and all abortion clinics and redirect it to authentic healthcare providers who helped save lives instead of ending them. Even though pro-abortion politicians controlled the Senate and the White House, the House could refuse to approve any budget that allowed funding for abortion clinics. Yet, House members were afraid to do that. If the government shut down over abortion funding, the media would blame them, and they knew it.

"It will be on the front page of *Politico* that the Republicans shut down the government," said the chief of staff nervously, angry that we were making such a big ask of his boss. I wondered how someone that powerful could be so scared. The front page of *Politico*? Who cares? How many people even read *Politico*, anyway? Was *Politico* running the country now? I believed that constituents wanted to see courage and leadership displayed, not cowardice and submission, to a hostile media.

Increasingly, our team discovered the necessity of reaching people directly with our stories and videos and not relying on media to report on our findings. We worked to reach as many people as possible with our investigations of the abortion industry's abuses. We also continued developing our own independent reporting arm, Live Action News, to cover stories about abortion and other threats to human dignity, as well as the political battles about both.

After the sex-trafficking investigation, our next project focused on sex-selective abortion. The cultural preference for sons worldwide has led to millions of abortions of female babies. Although the problem is most severe in countries such as India and China, the United States is not immune. In 2012, we looked into the question of whether Planned Parenthood clinics would commit abortions on babies for no other reason than that the baby was female. To find out, our team went to clinics across the country, from Manhattan to Maui.

We named the campaign Protect Our Girls. In Austin, Texas, our investigator presented at a Planned Parenthood clinic as pregnant. Claiming to want only a son, she was encouraged by a staffer to have a late-term abortion if tests proved the baby female. In New York City, a staffer working at a clinic named for Margaret Sanger counseled our investigator on how she could verify her child's sex and scheduled her for an abortion in case she was confirmed to be carrying a girl.

Arizona is one of the few states in the nation that has laws protecting preborn girls from sex-selective abortion. Committing such an abortion in Arizona is a felony. Staffers at Camelback Family Planning in Phoenix and the Women's Center in Tucson, however, did not take that law seriously. In Phoenix, the counselor coached a woman to lie on official paperwork to conceal the illegal abortion. At the Tucson facility, the surgical assistant did acknowledge the law. "We could lose our license," he told our investigator, but he nonetheless agreed to cover up a sex-selective abortion. "I'll just forget about it," he said. "But just be sure not to mention it." He did not even want the abortionist to know.

Upon learning of our investigator's stated motivation, a Planned Parenthood counselor in Maui told her that the reason for any abortion is "really up to" the mother. A Planned Parenthood staffer at the Honolulu facility opined that it was okay to get multiple sex-based abortions if the baby was not of the desired sex. In North Carolina, a Raleigh clinician actually encouraged our investigator to get a sex-selective abortion, even coached her on how to cover up her motives. If more than one abortion were needed to get the desired result, this clinician was happy to be of service. Staffers in nearby Chapel Hill, North Carolina, confirmed that they, too, would facilitate gender-biased abortions.

We had hoped that women sympathetic to feminism would respond to these results. And some did. But not enough to create the political impact we needed. For years now, radical feminists have been ignoring the deep hypocrisies in the pro-abortion movement. Planned Parenthood's defense of sex-selective abortion should have been roundly condemned by all so-called feminists, but it wasn't. Most who consider themselves women's rights advocates also ignore the emotional and physical damage an abortion does to a woman. Despite their professed feminism, they care less about real flesh-and-blood women than they do about theoretical ones. To defend their neglect, they have tried to elevate abortion into a feminist ritual that men cannot hope to understand. "If men could get pregnant," said prominent feminist Gloria Steinem, "abortion would be a sacrament."[1]

For some feminists, it already is. According to Father Frank Pavone, feminist Ginette Paris described abortion as a "sacred act," a sacrifice to the Greek goddess Artemis. "Artemis stands for the refusal to give life if the gift is not pure and untainted," wrote Paris. "As Artemis might kill a wounded animal rather than allow it to limp along miserably, so a mother wishes to spare the child a painful destiny."[2]

Another horrific practice Planned Parenthood defended was the refusal to provide medical care to babies who survived abortion attempts. Instead, abortionists such as Kermit Gosnell would simply kill the babies who survived, breaking existing prohibitions against infanticide. Abortion groups hated laws that reinforced prohibitions against these murders. In our next investigation, we tried to wake people up to the horror of abortion by exposing the killing of near-viable babies. The humanity of babies slaughtered in late-term abortions is obvious and undeniable. Infants born prematurely at the same age and in the same hospital routinely survive and grow healthy. Media groups often celebrate their homecomings.

In 2002, President George W. Bush signed into law the Born Alive Infants Protection Act. Under the law, children who survive a partial-birth or third trimester abortion are guaranteed constitutional protection. Those children even have the full rights of citizenship. Despite the law, however, these infants have on numerous occasions been left to die, struggling for life with each fading breath.

In this investigation, which we called Inhuman, we caught abortionists on camera admitting they would refuse such infants life-saving medical care. In Washington, DC, the manager of an abortion clinic promised our courageous, pregnant investigator that he would abort her twenty-two-week-old baby and leave the baby to die if the child survived the procedure.

In Phoenix, our investigator was also actually pregnant. The clinic checked the baby's age by ultrasound and determined that the baby was twenty-four weeks old, a week too old for a legal abortion in Arizona. Ever helpful, the clinic did a second ultrasound and determined that the baby was not twenty-four weeks old but, lo and behold, only twenty-three. The clinic agreed to kill the baby. To put the mom's mind at ease, the counselor reassured her that the clinic would not resuscitate a child who survived an abortion procedure.

In the Bronx, a pregnant investigator went to ask for an abortion. The clinician admitted that the baby was six months along and fully grown, too old at the time for an abortion at that facility. Again, trying to be helpful, she told the investigator to "flush it" or "put it in a bag or something" if the baby were delivered at home. Counselors often use the word *it*, even when referring to fully viable babies.

An abortion clinic in Bellevue, Nebraska, directed two pregnant investigators, twenty-two and twenty-six weeks along respectively, to its sister clinic in Maryland, a state that has no laws protecting preborn babies at this age. The clinic's abortionist/proprietor, Leroy Carhart, casually told the mothers that the abortion would cause the baby to get "soft, like mushy so you push it through." In an effort to lighten the moment, the abortionist compared the delivery of the deceased baby to "putting meat in a crock-pot." If the dead child were not delivered completely, the abortionist joked, he would remove the child "in pieces," using "a pickaxe" and "a drill bit."

In New Mexico, a pregnant investigator approached a clinic about a two-day late-term abortion procedure. The abortion workers acknowledged the humanity of the preborn child, yet callously confirmed that they'd kill the child in utero through the induction abortion procedure to avoid delivering a "live baby." They warned her that if she went into labor prematurely, she must not dial 911 but instead deliver the child alone, into a toilet, while she waited for the abortionist to arrive.

We released these horrific, heart-wrenching videos. They were even more painful to produce than to watch. Our scenarios had been fictional; the brave women investigating the facilities loved their children fiercely.

But we all knew that in each investigative visit, there were dozens of women with precious sons and daughters in their wombs, offering their children up for excruciating dismemberment and slaughter. Other pro-life groups worked with members of Congress to introduce a bill prohibiting abortions after twenty weeks. I knew that as long as taxpayer funds continued to pay for the abortion industry's atrocities and prop up their political power, bills such as these would languish in one subcommittee or another. Congress needed to muster up the will to stop funding abortion providers, period.

We kept the pressure on while continuing to build alliances with other constituencies. Our next investigation took a different track. We hoped to warn parents about the impact of Planned Parenthood on young teenagers through its almost ubiquitous school-based sex education. We sent investigators who looked like young teenage girls to two clinics in Colorado, as well as clinics in Indiana, Minnesota, and Oregon. The girls asked for sex advice. What they got was stunning: tutorials in painful, risky sadomasochistic sex games, directions to shops that sold sex toys, and advice about how valuable it is for girls to watch hard-core pornography. Many parents were outraged, and some used our videos at school councils to convince administrators to block the abortion groups from giving presentations to students.

Our investigations revealed Planned Parenthood's ideology of blind and unwavering support for abortion. So much for "choice" and "women's health." It was as if Planned Parenthood had indoctrinated its staffers to spare them all moral qualms when closing the deal on an abortion. Abortion because the baby is Black? Totally acceptable. Abortion because the baby is a girl? No problem. Abortion because the baby is imperfect? Of course. By refusing to acknowledge that abortion killed a human being, these staffers could justify abortion for any reason—or no reason at all.

Despite the massive media and financial advantage Planned Parenthood and its allies had, they were not winning the battle for the public's hearts and minds. We and our allies were making incremental progress. In 2006, before we launched our first investigation into Planned Parenthood, 41 percent of Americans considered themselves pro-life. By 2013, that number had increased to 48 percent,[3] despite Planned Parenthood's control of the White House and the media.

While our team at Live Action passionately worked to build our movement's momentum, I wrestled to find a lifestyle that would prevent me from succumbing to burnout. On planes every week, I traveled to almost all fifty states and flew around the world to speak, advocate, and build a team. I loved traveling, but I knew that this way of life was not sustainable long-term without breaks. The more responsibility I had, the harder it became for me to make new friends close to my age. The conservative, pro-life circle in DC felt suffocatingly small at times. When I broke up with a boyfriend, I risked losing the group of friends we shared. It was also hard to be friends with the people who worked for me. I was their boss, after all. My mentors helped. Their coaching helped. Finding a small group of friends who understood the burden of the cause and who became a safe place to laugh, to cry, and to struggle with helped. Praying helped even more, but I felt my own inadequacies daily.

Being a public figure, I learned, can bring extra romantic attention. This causes its own stress. The attention felt flattering at times, but when that attention inspired stalkers, it became nightmarish. Twice, I was followed in my car by random men. Others repeatedly contacted me on social media and sent gifts and flowers to Live Action's PO Box or showed up at my publicized events. When well-meaning acquaintances asked to set me up with people they knew, it was hard to know where to draw the line. And even among the more normal guys I met at parties or bars or through friends, there was sometimes a ladder-climber dynamic, an unfortunate but often true DC stereotype. The lure of power and success that pervaded the city seemed to have hooked many of my peers.

In a city as surreal as Washington, it was the everyday reality that threatened to wear me down the most: the inertia, the power struggles, and the apathy. It's naïve to think that progress is uniform and momentum is unstoppable. While there will be moments of breakthrough, most often the work is simply a slog. When you stand up for what is right, even among allies, you will face obstacles. The opposition has a will of its own, and they will push back. But to force the necessary change, you have to keep the pressure on. You have to persevere.

Fortitude is perseverance in spite of difficulties, especially the private difficulties that no one sees. Like any virtue, fortitude is a muscle that requires practice, those small, daily, grueling repetitions to build our strength. The little day-to-day battles may not seem like much in the greater scheme of our work, but faithfully fighting them will grow our capacity to face the bigger ones. Fortitude is key to any great endeavor, and the only way to earn it is one small step at a time.

No cause is without obstacles; expect them. And no battle is won without perseverance; stay the course and never give up.

CHAPTER 19

Make a Mistake, Get Up Again

I was back in the hot seat at headquarters, and there were moments when the anxiety felt crippling. I was managing dozens of people, raising millions of dollars, and giving hundreds of media interviews and speeches in an effort to shut down the nation's biggest abortion chain, and yet, it never felt like enough. And there was so much room for error.

It was all so much simpler when I first started. Back then, I would simply take the next right step, pray on the sidewalk outside a clinic, volunteer at a pregnancy center, or do activism on my college campus. It felt more immediate. It felt like I was personally making the difference in that moment. It felt much more rewarding than giving a speech about how other people should take action when my action in that moment was just giving a speech.

And there was much less risk when I was first starting out. There's a simplicity about having no money and being a college student that few people expect much from. But now that I was the head of a nationally recognized nonprofit, a boss, and a leader in our movement, any mistakes I made hurt that much more.

But mistakes are inevitable. The key is that we get up again.

To promote the Protect Our Girls investigation, Live Action worked with a PR company and a few other pro-life groups to put together a press conference at which a dozen or so members of Congress would speak. A number of representatives were pushing legislation to ban abortions done because of the sex, race, or health of the baby, and our investigation was an opportunity for them to win support for their bill. The press conference was to be held on the lawn outside the Capitol building at 8:00 a.m.

I set my alarm for six o'clock but ended up hitting the snooze button multiple times. Finally, at 6:30 a.m., I pulled myself out of bed and scrambled to get ready, then ran out the door to call a cab. It seemed like everything that could go wrong did go wrong on the way to the press conference. I arrived at 8:02 a.m. A crowd of Congress members stood by the podium, and several media crews and cameras hovered impatiently nearby. I walked up to the congressman who had introduced the new legislation to ban sex-selective abortions and said hello.

Everyone was just waiting. It suddenly dawned on me that they were waiting for me to start the press conference. I thought the congressman was hosting it, but I realized with a wave of horror that I was expected to host.

"Are you going to emcee?" he asked.

"I can," I said, hesitantly. "But would you prefer to?"

"I'm fine doing it but whatever you think," he said, a little flustered. "I'll do whatever you think!"

"Okay, go ahead," I responded.

The congressman took the podium and started talking. The press conference went smoothly enough from there. Once we finished our statements, we took questions from the press and made small talk until everyone disbanded.

Afterward, I hopped in a cab with our communications director and we headed to our little office. A few hours later, I received a phone call. It was from a former congresswoman who worked for another advocacy group that was at the press conference.

"Lila," she said bluntly, "you cannot walk into your own press conference late. That is such unprofessional behavior. It is unacceptable. All those Congress members were there for you, and you were the last one to show up!"

At first, I was taken aback. I didn't know what to say. Then I pulled myself together and mumbled, "Thank you so much for the feedback." I quickly realized she was right. While I felt humiliated, I also knew this was going to help me grow. If she hadn't taken the time to tell me that my lateness reflected poorly on me and our work, I would not have had such an explicit learning moment. Thanks to her intervention, I made sure that I was always on time for subsequent events. That meant getting up earlier, knowing in advance where I was going, and making sure there was margin in my schedule in case something went wrong. I also made sure my staff and any companies we worked with knew exactly what to expect and plan for at future events.

Of course, after this faux pas, part of me wanted to disqualify myself from doing a press conference ever again. But I realized that when we make a mistake, real humility comes not by running from the mistake but by admitting our failure and then addressing the issue so we will do better in the future. We need to allow our mistakes to teach us so we can better teach others. In the same way, we need to be patient with the mistakes of others. "Canceling" ourselves or others removes all opportunity for change and growth.

In my case, no one else was doing what Live Action was doing, and the world needed more, not fewer, activists, even if we were imperfect. We will all make mistakes, perhaps not as public as showing up late for a congressional press conference, but we cannot let our failures derail us. Using a failure as a reason to stop trying is a cop-out. Let's let our mistakes teach us humility but never use them as excuses to give up trying. The stakes are too high to take yourself out of the fight. Your cause needs you. Keep going.

PART 3

COMING HOME

CHAPTER 20

Learn to Pivot

Learning to pivot is an essential skill. A pivot in an organization or a movement is a definitive change in strategy or direction after new information reveals the existing approach is ineffective, for one reason or another. A pivot may even include reassessing the original goal of the company—the problem they had set out to solve or the product they had begun to build—and exchanging it for a better one.

In any enterprise, we have to test things to see if they work and understand that what may have worked in the past will not necessarily work in the future. And that's okay. We should never fall in love with our tools or our tactics. Focus and experience will prove whether or not they work, and if they aren't working, it's time to pivot. Our game plan and tactics should always be placed in service of the cause.

For the first seven years, Live Action focused on investigative reporting. That was the tactic we used to expose the abortion industry and Planned Parenthood's willingness to enable the sexual abuse of minors, the racism of would-be donors, the sexual trafficking of young girls, the sexual miseducation of teens, the gruesomeness of the late-term abortion industry, and sex-selective abortion, among other evils. In this process, we revealed the lies routinely told by Planned Parenthood staff and management to cover their crimes.

Many of our investigations gave us the opportunity to demonstrate how abusive and lawless Planned Parenthood has been. When our videos went viral and got media coverage, our investigations brought abortion into the forefront of public awareness. As a result of our investigative reporting, more than a dozen states cut off Planned Parenthood from various taxpayer-funded sources. Several of those states opened investigations into the abortion chain's practices. Severed from state funding, dozens of Planned Parenthood facilities closed, and multiple staff were fired for embarrassing the corporation.

But that was state money. Planned Parenthood now has an annual revenue in excess of $1.4 billion, more than $600 million of which comes from the federal government in one form or another.[1] Our work had moved the House to vote for defunding Planned Parenthood, but the Senate and White House would not yield. Planned Parenthood had deep pockets and friends in high places, in both the political and media spheres. Its media friends included most journalists and many entertainers, and they continued to influence millions to support abortion.

Few mainstream media reporters were interested in reporting on our investigative findings. Often, to the extent mainstream media investigated anything we did, it was in an attempt to discredit us. They were not interested in asking real questions about the operations of the nation's biggest abortion chain or the abuses of independent abortion facilities. Meanwhile, the social media giants—from Facebook to Twitter to Pinterest—often discriminated against us, shutting us down or limiting our exposure.

It seemed as though most people who supported abortion didn't care about Planned Parenthood's other abuses, or they didn't trust us, as pro-life activists, to report the truth. I realized that, more than ever, we needed to help change minds on abortion before we could effectively change minds on Planned Parenthood. This didn't mean we should drop investigative reporting; Live Action still continues it today and will expose the abuses of the abortion industry until the industry is shut down. But I realized that investigative reporting and lobbying were not enough on their own.

We were never going to give up, but we were going to pivot. Instead of releasing a major investigation, Live Action's brilliant creative team planned a new video campaign. Working with a former abortionist, Dr. Anthony Levatino, we began creating videos that would show the reality of abortion. The videos were detailed medical animations of the four most prevalent abortion procedures from the first trimester through the third.

Dr. Levatino had committed more than twelve hundred abortions before he experienced a dramatic conversion. In the midst of a dilation and evacuation (D&E) abortion, he had a moment of clarity so intense it made him nauseous. "For the first time in my career . . . I really looked at that pile of body parts on the side of the table," he stated. "And I didn't see her wonderful right to choose. And I didn't see what a great doctor I was helping [the woman] with her problem. And I didn't even see the $800 cash I just made in fifteen minutes. All I could see was somebody's son or daughter."[2] In his eyes, the fetus he had just aborted suddenly became a human being.

Live Action's pivot proved to be a powerful one. Within months of release, more than forty million people had watched our medical animation videos online, with thousands of people commenting on how the videos had changed their minds on abortion.

As we were releasing the abortion procedure videos, I watched Planned Parenthood, its political allies, and the media combine to smash another serious threat to their kingdom of lies. Using techniques he had helped to develop at Live Action, David Daleiden, now leading his own advocacy organization, launched an investigation into Planned Parenthood's trafficking in the organs and tissue of preborn children.

Posing as buyers for a profit-driven medical research company, David and another activist, Sandra Merritt, gained the confidence of Planned Parenthood clinicians in several states and captured on camera staggering proof that Planned Parenthood was indeed violating federal law, crassly profiting from illegal organ trafficking, deceiving women into signing consent forms, and even altering medical procedures to obtain more usable baby parts.

David started releasing his videos in July 2015. At this point, Live Action already had the largest social media following of any pro-life or pro-abortion group, as well as one of the largest activist databases. Working alongside David, we helped publicize the horrific findings to tens of millions of people. The videos were wrenching. It was horrific to watch a clinician pick through a tray of a murdered baby's body parts while talking about their commercial value.

The videos sent a shock wave through Washington. At one point, the *New York Times* found itself speculating as to whether "the new offensive will succeed in crippling Planned Parenthood."[3] Even Hillary Clinton, then the Democratic frontrunner for president and a dedicated Planned Parenthood supporter, was worried. "I have seen pictures from [the videos] and obviously find them disturbing," Clinton told a reporter that July.[4]

Then Planned Parenthood struck back. It got prosecutors in Houston and in California to bring trumped-up charges against David and Sandra. At the same time that California's then-Attorney General Kamala Harris initiated her investigation, she was accepting money from Planned Parenthood for her Senate campaign. But who noticed?

For all the powerful facts these videos presented, the effort to defund, if not to prosecute, Planned Parenthood for its illegal activities fell short. By the time the 2016 election season rolled around, Planned Parenthood felt confident enough to ridicule David and Sandra as criminals and their videos as fake.[5] What was criminal was Planned Parenthood's illegal sale of baby body parts, not the brave reporting of the ones who exposed them.

Despite a House committee and Senate panel designated to investigate the videos further, no legislative action was taken. Planned Parenthood dodged the bullet by claiming, in the words of its president, Cecile Richards, that the money charged "is not a fee. It's not a fee. It's actually just the cost of transmitting this material."[6] Material? Even after the exposé, because of the support of their pro-abortion allies in Congress, Planned Parenthood continued to receive more than $1.5 million *a day* from taxpayers.

Watching all of this happen, watching David accomplish something this impactful, then seeing America's abortion culture absorb the blow and move on seemingly unscathed was a significant factor in Live Action's decision to pivot. I realized again how deeply entrenched the abortion culture was in the media and in our political system.

At the same time, I was seeing how powerful and effective the abortion medical animation series had been in educating young people, much as Live Action had done in the early years. I knew that our solution had to be more than just political. It had to be personal. It had to begin in the consciences and imaginations of people across the nation. To change our laws, we would have to change hearts.

It wasn't that I hadn't known the importance of changing public opinion up to that point. All our investigative reporting had helped to change minds. But I saw more clearly than ever that even the most explosive investigative reports on the abortion industry were simply not enough. While continuing investigative reporting, we also had to focus our efforts on grassroots strategies. We had to go beyond battling the abortion industry and work to shift public opinion on abortion itself. We needed people to see abortion as the ultimate crime.

Washington, I realized, was not the place to reimagine our crusade. Our work there felt downright Sisyphean. No matter how far we pushed our rock up Capitol Hill, there was always some powerful force ready to push it right back down. Without a pivot, I felt like we would never get it to the top. DC wasn't going to change itself. Transformation needed to come from outside the nation's capital city, with millions of voices demanding change. We could keep a presence in DC, but the true location of our movement was in the hearts and souls of the public—and they needed inspiration and direction.

I didn't know all the repercussions of our decision then, but within a few years of our pivot, we would dramatically multiply Live Action's impact and help our movement achieve historic gains. As our focus shifted to education and grassroots campaigns, our videos, articles, and social media content would be viewed by millions of people daily and help inspire an unprecedented groundswell of pro-life legislation and policy. By 2019, the abortion rate in America would drop to a historic low.

My heart was also pulling me back home. I was homesick for California, and it felt like now was time to return. As I packed up my apartment, I decided I would take as few things as possible. I didn't want to deal with the burden of having boxes and boxes of belongings and paying to ship everything home. I wanted to simplify what I had so I could be mobile and agile. I decided I'd move back to the Bay Area for several months to spend time with family. Then I would head to Los Angeles to open a new Live Action office and focus the fight on changing hearts and minds.

CHAPTER 21

Love the Ones You're Given

To defeat Planned Parenthood and the abortion industry, I knew we had to explain what abortion really is directly to the world. That required talking honestly about how abortion ends the life of a child, about the harm it does to women and girls, and about the damage it does to men and families as well. But we also had to be able to offer a better vision, one in which every life is loved and protected—and I knew that vision had to start close to home. It had to start with me.

Over time, it became increasingly clear that if pursuing my work caused me to neglect the people God had put in my life, I was doing something wrong. It mattered how well I loved and treated the people closest to me. It mattered, too, how I received God's love and grew in my faith. This was a lesson I first learned early on in my activism work.

When I was a sophomore in high school, a friend and I decided to stage a major fundraising gala to raise relief funds for famine victims in Niger. Our timeline was short. The international community had largely ignored the crisis. The money we raised could mean life or death for families. We already had a contract with an international relief organization that was prepared to fly in lifesaving nutrition supplies if we could raise the money in time to pay for the food and flight.

In addition to juggling classes and homework, I was pulling late nights to make this event happen and to get people to attend and donate. Some nights, I returned home after ten o'clock, which was technically my curfew on school nights. One evening, I walked in and barely said hello to my parents before rushing up the stairs to my bedroom. "Lers," my dad called from the living room, using one of my family's favorite nicknames for me. "Can you come chat for a minute?"

"Sure, Dad," I said and sat down in a cozy armchair.

"We love what you are doing," he said gently but matter-of-factly. "But we are concerned about how you're doing it. You're not here for dinners with the family. You're rarely here during most of the weekend. We're your family not your hotel."

I felt a little defensive, but I knew he was right. There had been several nights when my mom had asked if I would be joining for dinner, but I said no. I hadn't been around. I had been too busy. Looking back, I'm grateful my dad called me out on that. It reoriented the way I looked at my work.

No matter how important I felt my work was, that did not give me a pass to ignore my family or leave them to do my chores. The people in my family, the people I lived with, deserved my time, presence, and help. They had their own needs, their own desires for connection, their own struggles and hopes and joys. Was I present to them? Or was I so busy with my own work, no matter how important I thought it was, that I was ignoring the eternal souls right before my eyes?

When we are working toward a higher goal or fighting for an important cause, it can be easy to justify cutting corners in the way we care for the people closest to us. But to build our character and practice true love, we must be faithful to the ones with whom we've been entrusted. Moving back to California after years in DC gave me more opportunities to do just that.

I'm forever grateful that my parents gave me seven siblings, and my brothers and sisters are some of my favorite companions. They have taught me so much about the preciousness of family, about acceptance and friendship. They have also given me some amazing nieces and nephews. My relationship with my sister Caterina in particular has taught me about love, especially in the face of the unexpected and unknown.

On Cat's eighteenth birthday, I was home from Washington for a few days to visit my family. When I asked her where she wanted to eat lunch, she suggested Denny's. It had also been my favorite restaurant as a teenager. I especially appreciated those late-night dinners with friends after concerts or pro-life activism.

Cat sat across from me. We ordered pancakes and an omelet. Breakfast for lunch. Cat was restless, occasionally commenting, "I need a cigarette." I asked about her classes. I asked a few questions about her love life. Apparently, she was dating a guy who was not treating her well. Her hair was the fourth different color I had seen in the last ten months, black this time. She had also gotten another piercing since I last saw her. I asked if it hurt, and she laughed.

The external signs—the cigarettes, the piercings, the hair—troubled me less than her mental health, what was going on within. I knew she wasn't happy. She was not practicing any faith, and I knew she struggled with anxiety.

I decided to change the subject and asked her about horseback riding. This question resonated. Horses seemed to be the only thing about which she was truly passionate. But throughout our lunch, the conversation was strained. She picked at her pancakes unenthusiastically. I knew she was anxious about the calories.

I probed gently, trying to get her to share more about what was going on inside her heart. She stared at me blankly. "Sis," she said, her emotional numbness all too apparent, "I don't really want to talk about *stuff*." We both knew what she meant. The conversation was over.

Nine months later, I received news about Cat that had me rushing home to California from a speaking event in Oregon. After the plane landed, one of my younger brothers picked me up, and we headed right to the hospital. I stepped off the hospital elevator and faced the closed, cold white double doors of the ICU. They were locked, and a small sign posted outside read, "No visitors for the next thirty minutes. Shift change."

Through the crack in the door, I could see down the long, sterile corridor. Cat was in there, somewhere. I rang the intercom repeatedly and started to choke up as I asked again for someone to let me in. Finally, the familiar face of my older brother appeared on the other side of the door. He pulled it open and let me in. We hurried down the hall and into a dark side room. As my eyes adjusted, I saw my sister lying on the bed. The IV in her arm delivered the antidote to the bottle of pills she had swallowed the day before.

Cat looked younger than her eighteen years and more vulnerable. Her tousled, purple-dyed hair fell in tangled strands onto her face. She raised a hand in a weak greeting, "Hi, Li." Relief flooded my heart, and I burst into tears.

"Cat, I'm so glad you're okay."

"I've got nine lives." She smiled wryly.

I held her hand and sat there, tears falling.

"I'm sorry, Sis," I choked out. "I'm so sorry. I love you so much."

Cat pushed the hair off her face and sat up a little straighter in bed.

"Sis," she asked quietly. "Do you have a hair tie? Would you mind French-braiding my hair?"

Through my tears, I slowly, awkwardly began the braid. I'd never been good at braiding hair. Caterina had always been the crafty one, the one good with her hands and skilled at styling hair. After fumbling for a few minutes, I managed a lopsided braid, relieved there was no mirror for her to see how off-kilter it was. She looked ahead peacefully, her eyes slowly closing as she drifted into sleep.

■

Caterina has always loved horses. She worked for a few months at a small horse ranch by a beach near San Francisco. Whenever she could, she rode her favorite horse bareback down the cliffs onto the sand so she could gallop by the ocean, her hair flying in the wind. That was my little sister, daring to the point of recklessness, full of zeal for life.

It had been nearly two months since that night in the hospital, and now my sister Nina and I were hurrying down a rural Tennessee road to join Cat at another horse ranch, this time a residential treatment facility that helped people recover from eating disorders and other mood comorbidities. Cat's zeal for life had been drained away in the weeks and months leading up to her suicide attempt. I prayed that the patience, loyalty, and instinctive life force of the horses at the treatment center would help restore it. Cat had been there for almost five weeks. We were meeting her for a family therapy weekend.

Once at the ranch, we met Cat among a group of about fifty other patients and their families in a main hall. She looked great: she'd already added several pounds to her too-thin frame, and the light was coming back into her eyes. We three sisters hugged.

"How has it been going, Sis?" I asked.

"Really good," she said. "You'll really like the sessions today."

There were about forty attendees at this family encounter session. We all sat in plastic chairs at round tables. A staff therapist opened the session.

"It's so important to find the cause that's greater than ourselves," the therapist explained.

The cause! I thought. Suddenly, I was nine again, remembering how I first encountered my cause. Maybe I was too young, maybe my parents should have done a better job of hiding that abortion book. But without that book—and so many other providential moments—I was not sure I would have found my cause. And had I not found my cause, I am not sure I would have overcome my own demons, discovered myself, or discovered God. My cause had filled my life with purpose in some of my darkest moments. It reminded me that life, this precious, fragile life we've each been given, is always worth fighting for.

We broke into groups by family. The therapist handed us a large sheet of brown paper with a blank family tree on it. Our job was to insert the dysfunctions of family members we knew or had been told about, going as far back in the generations as possible, and to use various symbols to indicate those dysfunctions. Nina, Cat, and I went to work filling in roles and symbols: suicide, addiction, divorce, mental illness, abuse. Within an hour, our tree was thick with the symbols of dysfunction.

Our family tree showed a clear pattern of human failure, the sins of one generation affecting the next generation. And there we were at the bottom of the tree, with those wounds now visible on so many branches.

Nina, Cat, and I talked through our family tree together. There were tears but most of all a sense of hope. We now had a better understanding what our family of origin had been through. We also understood how the wounds of our grandparents had directly impacted our parents, and, inevitably then, our own childhoods. My mother would tell us as we were growing up, "Every generation has the chance to do better than the generation before. We just hope you kids do better than me and your father."

I always understood her to mean that she wanted us to be healthier, happier, and more successful than they were. Most parents want that. But I now realized more deeply the yearning of their hearts. They wanted us to be healthier, happier, and more successful, but even more so, they wanted us to break the cycles of dysfunction and pain in our family—they wanted it to stop with them. And while they didn't have all the answers for how to heal the wounds in our family, they did their best to transmit to us kids every ounce of what they did know. Sometimes the solutions they improvised created their own harm, but more often than not, they succeeded in making our lives better. And my parents tried, passionately, to create something beautiful and new for their family, doing their best to pull from everything good and wise and loving in their own upbringings.

I realized with an overwhelming gratitude that just as specific wounds could influence the behaviors of one generation to wound the next, so could that generation's choices to pursue healing. To choose faith. To choose love.

Our family trees filled in, we all shuffled outside into the afternoon light toward a firepit. The therapist asked the assembled families to come forward one by one and burn their maps in the pit. We watched a few families take their turn.

"Who wants to go next?" the therapist asked.

With our rolled-up family-of-origin tree in hand, Caterina stepped forward.

"I am burning depression, sexual abuse, anxiety, and addiction," she announced. The chart flared as she dropped it into the fire.

We had brought our family dysfunction into the light—we had named it. Now we could grieve over it. Together, we were committed to overcoming our inherited bad habits of thought and deed. We could change our lives, and we could redirect the trajectory of our family. As we watched the flames lick the map, we three sisters stood there quietly and put our arms around one another. The family map, with all its symbols of pain, burned brightly, then flamed out, collapsing into embers.

That night, as Nina slept in a twin bed next to mine in our guest cabin, I thought back over the events of the day. I marveled at Cat's life, this little sister I had begged God to give me as a young girl. She and Nina were among the best gifts of my life—all my siblings were. What was God doing with our family? I knew that through our family's pain we were discovering more about ourselves and one another than we even knew there was to discover. Our understanding would bring grief, but it would also bring healing and freedom. Listening to the quiet hum of the cabin air conditioner, I drifted off to sleep, consoled by the bright hope of that freedom.

We've all been entrusted with people to love: grandparents, parents, siblings, children, extended family, or friends who have come to rely on us like family. Does someone feel lonely or unloved? Do our loved ones feel heard and seen and appreciated? Do they know that we care, that we are there for them, that we will fight for them? It can be easy to become consumed in our work, especially at those times when we experience great momentum and feel we are making progress. It can also be easy to forget our loved ones during the harder times in our work, when we may face tremendous obstacles and struggle to keep going. No matter what we are going through in our fight to make the world better, faithfully loving those around us, as imperfect as our love may be, is a constant call. We also need the love our families have to give us, however imperfect it may be. We can achieve the greatest victories in our activism, we can stand up to terrible evils and speak great truths, but if we reject or ignore those closest to us, have we really succeeded?

To love our families means we must also pursue healing in our families. Love means making time for one another, celebrating each other's joys, and embracing each other when we hurt. Healing can mean having the hard conversations when necessary, saying sorry for our failings, and being quick to forgive. It can mean getting outside help too. Our causes require sacrifice, but our families deserve our sacrifice too.

A family open to love, that seeks healing and strives to grow together, is the secret to a changed and renewed world. As we fight for our causes, may we never stop fighting to love our families best.

CHAPTER 22

Embrace Mercy

In a story told in the gospel of John, the Pharisees drag a woman accused of adultery before Jesus. Hoping to trap Jesus in a violation of Mosaic law, they say, "Now in the law Moses commanded us to stone such women. Now what do you say?" Infinitely wiser than those who would try to ensnare him, Jesus responds, "Let anyone among you who is without sin be the first to throw a stone at her." Chastened, the Pharisees slink away, and Jesus says to the woman, "Neither do I condemn you. Go your way, and from now on do not sin again" (John 8:5, 7, 11 NRSVCE).

Jesus is not telling us to refrain from judgment. Rather, he is instructing us to temper our judgment with mercy and understanding, never forgetting that we, too, are sinners. Those of us fighting for any cause have to be continually reminded of this message. Just as we do not wish to be driven away, we should not drive away even the most prodigal of sinners. Instead, we extend mercy and pray for their return because we know God has been merciful to us. We recognize that just as others need forgiveness, we need it too.

It is all too easy to fall into the hypocrisy of pointing out the sins of others while ignoring our own. Jesus had no patience for this: "You hypocrite," he said, "first take the log out of your own eye, and then you will see clearly to take the speck out of your neighbor's eye" (Matthew 7:5 NRSVCE). It takes profound humility to accept mercy for the sins we commit. We have to acknowledge that they were sins in the first place, and admitting our own wrongdoing is painful. Admitting sin can drum up feelings of guilt and shame. But if we ignore the guilt we feel, we will never be free of it. Guilt—when we pay attention to it—can be a gift. It is our conscience prodding us to turn away from doing wrong and choose the good instead.

Every woman and man who chooses to abort their child has committed a grave sin. We cannot excuse the sin, but it is never our place to condemn the sinner, because we, too, are fellow sinners. And just as it's not our place to condemn others, neither is it our place to condemn ourselves. Jesus wants to extend mercy to all of us, no matter what we've done, if only we will receive it. There is no sin, no mistake, and no fall too great for God to forgive.

Just as we've received the liberating gift of God's mercy, we should pray for that mercy to be accepted by others who may be living in blindness. Sometimes those prayers are answered in powerful ways. For three years, Ramona Treviño worked as the manager of a Planned Parenthood abortion referral facility in Sherman, Texas. After the Live Action videos from the Mona Lisa project and sex trafficking investigations went public, Planned Parenthood publicly announced they would be retraining all eleven thousand staffers around the country, ostensibly to help them weed out and report sexual predators. Ramona was one of those who received the training. To her dismay, she learned that the training had little to do with helping underage girls or following state laws that required abuse reports.

Summoning up her courage, Ramona asked the trainer, "I guess what I'm wondering is, what do we as managers do if something like this really does happen at our clinics. How can we be prepared so that if it does happen, we can make sure our clients are safe and nothing illegal is going on?"

The trainer did not even attempt to disguise Planned Parenthood's real concern. "We're not here to discuss that, Ramona," she shot back. "We're here to identify whether we're being violated by an undercover operation."[1] That training session was another moment of conscience for Ramona, and soon she would quit Planned Parenthood and join the pro-life movement. Needless to say, she made a powerful witness.

I met Ramona Treviño for the first time when I interviewed her on film for Live Action in Los Angeles. Our team had flown Ramona in from Texas as part of one of our investigative reports, Abortion Corporation. Kind and soft-spoken, Ramona courageously sat down with me in front of multiple cameras to share her story with the world.

Later, Ramona would fly with me to Washington, DC, to walk the halls of Congress lobbying senators and representatives to strip the nation's largest abortion chain of its hundreds of millions of dollars of annual taxpayer subsidy. Standing side by side, we spoke with some of the most powerful elected politicians in the world and urged them to take action. We were no longer enemies but friends united in a common cause to fight for life. All by God's grace.

Ramona was not the first person in the abortion industry to see the light, and I am sure she will not be the last. Dr. Bernard Nathanson certainly saw it. As a practicing abortionist and an early leader of the abortion rights movement, he estimated he had presided over sixty thousand abortions as director of a facility and personally committed five thousand, including that of his own child.[2] With the development of ultrasound, he had a radical change of heart.

"I am one of those who helped usher in this barbaric age," Nathanson later confessed. Over time, he found his way from atheism to Catholicism for the reason that "no religion matches the special role for forgiveness that is afforded by the Catholic Church."[3] He knew he needed that forgiveness to be a truly effective spokesman for the pro-life cause. And the Catholic Church and other pro-life advocates celebrated his conversion and welcomed him to the cause.

Live Action regularly works with ex-abortionists and clinic workers to create our educational content. Dr. Anthony Levatino worked closely with our team to create the abortion procedures videos, now viewed more than one hundred million times. Dr. Levatino allowed God to transform his experience with abortion from a dark spot on his soul to a light that could illuminate the horrors of abortion for others. Now Dr. Levatino speaks internationally, advocating on behalf of children in the womb and their mothers. By accepting mercy himself, he gives others hope that they, too, can find forgiveness and freedom.

Over the years, I've met dozens of former abortionists and abortion clinic workers, but few have moved me the way retired OB/GYN Kathi Aultman did during our 2019 Live Action interview.[4]

Kathi had just started medical school at the University of Florida College of Medicine when *Roe v. Wade* was decided in January 1973. Caught up in the spirit of the times and believing "that women should have control over their own bodies," Kathi and her fellow medical students learned to perform abortions as a routine part of their medical training through residency. Dehumanization was built into their education. The doctors-in-training moved from chick embryos to human babies with minimal reflection. "I did not see them as human beings," Kathi said. "I just saw them as embryos and fetuses. Not as people."

Toward the end of her residency, Kathi herself got pregnant but continued to perform abortions, in part to prove her mettle as a woman of science in what was still a male-dominated field. The birth of her daughter made Kathi more reflective about the humanity of these babies but not enough to overcome her commitment to women's rights and her obligation as a doctor.

A series of three patients broke the spell. The first was a young woman whose babies Kathi had aborted three times prior. The second was a callous young woman who, when asked if she wanted to see the baby, snapped, "No. I just want to kill it." And the third was a married mother of four who wept copiously through the whole procedure knowing she was killing a child so as not to put a strain on family finances. That was Kathi's last abortion. She refused to do them after that.

Kathi's journey from abortionist to pro-life activist was a long and deliberate one. In her practice, she began to see women who had never recovered from the emotional damage of an earlier abortion. She became a Christian and began to marvel at the joyful young children she saw at church who might not have existed had the abortionist lobby had their way. Then she, like me, began to study the Holocaust, a subject with which she was familiar as her father had helped liberate the camps during World War II.

"They didn't see the Jews and the Gypsies and the others as people," said Kathi of the Nazis. "And if you don't consider someone human, you can do anything you want." Upon coming to this realization, a more frightening one gripped her. "That's when I realized I was a mass murderer," she said sadly. "I had killed all of these people. And that's when I completely changed my opinion on abortion."

The acceptance and love of her fellow Christians made all the difference in Kathi's emotional recovery. At a Christian healing center, she started down the road toward self-forgiveness. Normally reserved and professional, useful attributes in a doctor, Kathi let it all go. "I never understood what 'crying your eyes out' meant until that point," she said, "because I literally cried my eyes out and couldn't stop."

No one is beyond saving. There is no fall too far from the reach of God's mercy. As we fight for our cause and as we stand up for what's right, may mercy always mark our words, our thoughts, and our deeds. Never forget that those who have committed evil are capable of rejecting the evil they've done. In rejecting that evil, they may become the most compelling champions of the good. And one day, we may discover them fighting by our side.

CHAPTER 23

Learn to Grieve

Major turning points in our lives can sneak up on us. In 2015, this one did for me. I was on a red-eye flight to Brussels to speak before members of the EU Parliament about investigative reporting on Planned Parenthood. Planned Parenthood had a large international presence and even received money from the EU, so I hoped our research would inspire the EU to defund Planned Parenthood's European affiliates. I had a lot on my mind, and a nine-hour red-eye flight was bad enough. A middle seat just made it worse.

The previous few months had been a whirlwind. I had been working overtime to help publicize and defend the undercover work of my former employee and colleague, David Daleiden. I was planning my move back to California. And for added drama, I had recently broken up with a boyfriend.

Two hours after arrival in Brussels, I was scheduled to go straight to meetings at the European Parliament, so I needed to get some rest on the flight. Exhausted, I attempted sleep in my middle seat, but my head kept falling over onto my seatmate's shoulder. A balding Albanian man of forty or so, he spoke little English but had a kindly way about him. I, of course, spoke no Albanian.

As my head would start to graze his shoulder, I'd jolt awake, apologize profusely, and sit up straight again. Half-asleep and embarrassed,

I'd then nod off, only to wake up feeling mortified that I was once again snoozing on a stranger's shoulder. After a few rounds of this, the man tapped me on the arm, smiled kindly, and then pointed to his shoulder, "Okay, okay," he said reassuringly. I am no stranger to ulterior motives, but I was desperate and I could tell he felt truly sorry for me. Exhausted, I thanked him, mostly by nodding and smiling back, and then spent the last three hours of the flight awkwardly but gratefully dozing against the shoulder of a man I scarcely knew.

When I arrived in Belgium, I stumbled off the plane with my carry-on suitcase and hunted down a bathroom. Happily, I have always been quick to find one no matter how foreign the country. Debating for a few moments what to wear, I opted to keep on my boots—it was winter in Brussels, after all—and don a short-sleeve black dress. I washed my face, put in my contacts, applied some makeup, and headed outside to find a taxi.

The next day and a half went by quickly, beginning with back-to-back meetings with delegates who were determined to speak out against the abortion industry. They were a small group, but they were passionate about taking a stand. The next morning I gave a presentation to more delegates and met with community activists. After a long forty-eight hours with little sleep, I was exhausted. But I had one more stop, a dinner. A close friend of mine knew a couple, Paul and Branka, who helped run Hope Alive, an international organization spearheaded by a psychiatrist from Canada. Hope Alive was devoted to understanding and healing trauma from abortion and other forms of pregnancy loss, for parents as well as their surviving children.

I learned about the collateral trauma of abortion early in my career as an activist. While still at UCLA, I spoke at a fundraising event held on behalf of a large pregnancy care center. I shared my experiences as an undercover investigator and talked about my own commitment to the pro-life cause and how grateful I was for the sacrifice and dedication of the pregnancy care center's supporters. Afterward, dozens of the center's supporters approached me to take pictures with them. It felt strange to be called a hero, and it still does.

What affected me most, however, was one woman, probably in her fifties, who grasped my hands with tears in her eyes. "Thank you so much for what you do," she whispered. "I had an abortion when I was young, and there isn't a day that goes by when I don't think about my baby." My eyes filled with tears as she struggled to get out the next words. "I wish," she said, choking up, "I wish there had been someone to stop me, to tell me the truth. Thank you. Keep going. Never give up."

I knew there were millions of other women who felt as this woman did. But to see the raw pain still on her face and to feel the loss of her child wounded me to the core. Every abortion kills a child, but every abortion also damages a mother. More painful still, society tells her she has no reason to grieve. It wasn't a baby, after all. It was a choice. Some women bury their pain deeply, even denying it exists, but it manifests itself in other ways, sometimes decades later.

Over the years, I have heard from hundreds of women like the one at that fundraiser, women who tell me in hushed voices about the loss and guilt they still carry, often decades after their abortions. They want to be heard, to be acknowledged in their pain, to be able to share it, but they have so few outlets. These voices are brave and true and crucial. Hope Alive teaches that healing is possible after abortion, but first, the reality of what that abortion did—how it killed a baby, a precious son or daughter—must be reckoned with. The only way to heal is to allow ourselves to grieve. And the only way to grieve is to allow ourselves to hurt.

I have also found that there is a silent grief many fathers feel about their children lost to abortion. Sometimes for them that grief is compounded by shame and deep regret for the role they played in encouraging or paying for that abortion. They need healing too.

Were it not for the good work Paul and Branka did with post-abortion healing, I might have backed out of the visit. It was cold outside and already dark. Coming off a red-eye flight and two days full of meetings and presentations, I was eager to go back to my hotel and crash. After a few more appointments the next day, I would be returning to Washington.

Common sense told me to call it a day, but some inner voice told me to keep my meeting with this couple.

Paul and Branka lived in a Brussels suburb. I hailed another taxi and headed over the bumpy cobblestone streets to their apartment. It was a modest home, stacked above a garage, in a neighborhood about twenty minutes from Parliament. Once there, I climbed the stairs and rang the doorbell. The couple, with their nine-year-old son in tow, greeted me warmly. We settled down for a delicious dinner. I had almost forgotten how much I enjoyed having a home-cooked meal, even if it was at a stranger's home.

We didn't stay strangers for long. Within minutes, our conversation began to go deep. Most of us have met people with whom we instantly connect, people with whom we can speak freely about what's really on our hearts, about what really matters. That was Paul and Branka. Branka shared how she met Paul. She explained that she was raised in then-Communist Serbia and knew nothing of God. Faith was illegal. As an ambitious woman, she professed to hate men but secretly longed for a family, a family unlike the one in which she grew up. She never knew her father and felt only hostility from her mother, a woman who was openly cruel to her from her earliest days.

Branka would eventually become a Christian. Not one to hold back, she told God that she wanted him to send a husband right to her doorstep. It was a bold and specific prayer, but one that would be answered just as Branka requested. Months later, Paul showed up on her doorstep. He had been sent there to talk with her about a Christian missions group not knowing she was already a member.

Branka told me that all her life she had had nightmares in which her mother chased her with a knife, trying to kill her. She found out later in life that her mother had never wanted her and had even tried to abort her. Branka had to grieve her mother's rejection. Acknowledging all this became an essential part of Branka's healing.

Branka's story moved me deeply. I began to share stories of my own childhood. I loved my family fiercely, but growing up, there were difficult moments. Married young and with little community support in the early years, my parents struggled to find the skills and knowledge to navigate the complexities of a marriage and quickly growing family. In light of their own upbringing and personal challenges, I admire their courage to joyfully welcome all eight of their children. I am forever grateful for their love for us kids and the life they gave each of us. They worked tirelessly to give us their very best. To be sure, no one is perfectly prepared for parenthood. For so many reasons, I feel privileged to have been raised in my family. I look back on my childhood with gratitude for the faith, wisdom, and character my parents nurtured in us. My parents worked hard to have family dinners, to pray together as a family, to give us the best education possible and the opportunity for endless extracurriculars, including sports, music, speech, and debate. They opened their doors to Live Action in the earliest days and cheered on my siblings and me in many of our endeavors and interests. They chose to be generous when they could have chosen to take an easier path. But as with any family, there were struggles too.

As all children do, I craved my father's attention and affection. I still remember, for instance, the jolt of joy I felt as a five-year-old when my dad came home one night from work and announced he was going to take me on an ice cream date. But I also remember the painful sense of loss I felt when my dad was absent or angry, and I did not understand why, especially when I was on the cusp of adolescence. Raising a household of children and managing the pressures of work and school can be stressful for anyone, but these usual stresses were exacerbated by the mental health histories and the childhood wounds of my parents. On one side, my family struggled with OCD and anxiety; on the other, with depression. I inherited elements of both.

As the oldest girl, with five younger siblings, I internalized many of our family's burdens. Especially sensitive, I hated witnessing the fights between my dad and some of my brothers, and I hated conflict with either of my parents. I learned later that my dad's uncontrolled, often unpredictable outbursts largely came from his own struggle with depression, a disorder he hadn't yet gotten help for.

I wanted to shield my siblings from the conflict. And as much as I craved affection, I sometimes felt my mom and dad didn't see me. I often felt helpless—helpless to bring peace to my family, helpless to deal with the pain and anger inside of me. Meanwhile, my mother often sacrificed her own well-being as she poured herself out to manage the gang of us, and we could feel her anxiety.

I remember first pulling my hair in junior high school at about the time I lapsed into depression. My struggles were not obvious to others. I had a surface calm that cloaked the pain and anxiety I was feeling. At the time, I coped with the intensity of my life and the stress in my home by escaping into myself internally. I tried to work out of my own pain, pouring myself into my studies, my extracurriculars, and my work at Live Action. But without addressing the struggle inside me, this pattern could not hold, and I eventually started crumbling inside. I did not have the knowledge or tools to understand why I felt the way I felt.

The clinical name for compulsive hair-picking or pulling is Trichotillomania. It's a word I still have trouble pronouncing, and it is something I rarely talk about, even in private. I share it here to remind you that no matter what struggle you might be facing, no matter how shameful it may feel, freedom and health are possible. Trichotillomania is one of several body-focused repetitive disorders, some more or less severe. Some people pick compulsively at their nails or at their skin. In Trichotillomania, some actually pull out their hair, one hair at a time, by the roots. For me, the disorder took the form of relentlessly searching for split ends and pulling them off.

While living in DC, I was lonely and sometimes felt depressed. The high pressure of my work added to the stress, as did being in the public eye. It felt isolating to be a boss while still in my midtwenties, especially since most of my associates were older. The last two years had been especially hard. There were days when I just wanted to stay in bed. Other days, I spent picking at my hair.

Hesitantly at first, I shared my Trichotillomania struggle with Paul and Branka. Up to that point, I had spoken of this disorder only with my counselor. It felt so unusual, and in many ways shameful, that I was reluctant to talk about it even with friends.

Branka didn't flinch. She explained that the effects of trauma and stress can be retained in our bodies. These effects manifest themselves in different ways for people who have not dealt with the stress and healed from it. She explained that stress needed to be acknowledged, accepted, understood, and finally released.

Her words brought me so much consolation, resonating with me on an instinctual level. I realized as she spoke that I had never considered the need to grieve parts of my childhood. There had been so much good. My parents had worked so hard and had given us so much. Why would I grieve when there was so much good?

Because there had been hurt too. I had to look straight at the pain in my past and fully acknowledge it. I had to name the most painful and dysfunctional events, process them, and identify what should have happened instead. I had to imagine what should have been the healthy and loving alternative to the anger of my father, the fights with my brothers, the stress my mother faced. I had to allow myself to grieve, letting grief take whatever form came naturally to me. Such grief over the hurts and losses during childhood is not ingratitude. On the contrary, it allows us to understand more deeply what we have to be grateful for and to see the larger picture of our parents' struggles while still acknowledging the reality of the pain we've experienced.

Tired, but filled with hope and comfort, I left Paul and Branka's little home at 1:30 a.m. and headed back to my hotel. My first appointment wasn't until noon the next day so I knew I could sleep in. Once in my hotel room, I pulled the curtains shut, set an alarm for 11:00 a.m., and fell into a deep, peaceful sleep.

The next day, after two more meetings, I boarded my flight back to Washington, DC. Miraculously, I was upgraded to business class. Better still, I had a whole row to myself next to a window. In the comfort and privacy of that unexpected space, my grief found its outlet. I wept the whole flight home. I wept over the memories of hurt and isolation and longing. I also wept in thanksgiving for the great mystery of all that it had been my privilege to receive: the precious gift of my parents and my siblings and, with God's grace, the eternity we would spend glorifying him together with no more tears, only joy.

We can bring only as much healing to the world as we allow to take place in our hearts. As we grow, we discover new horizons of celebration and gratitude, and new depths of grief. Grieving our past and understanding it so we can accept both the right and wrong is the only pathway to healing.

In this life, we can't escape the evil and sin in our world, but we can forgive and reconcile. We can resolve to be better. The power of love, which comes from God, will never fail us.

CHAPTER 24

Find Your Heart

I stayed with my brother and sister-in-law and their four kids for a few months after I moved back to California. My nieces and nephew were ages one through five. After a trip away for speaking or meetings, or even after a trip to a local coffee shop, I would knock on the front door and hear their shouts and the tapping of four sets of little feet as they rushed to the entryway, shouting, "Auntie Lila's home!" "Hurray!" "Yippee!"

They vied with one another to be the first to greet me after their mom or dad unlocked the door. Their glee, their unadulterated sweetness in wanting to see me and be with me, brought me more joy and peace than anything my work could offer. They each embodied the very thing for which I was fighting: the beautiful gift of a child's life. I admired my brother and sister-in-law's commitment to embrace these little lives in all their messiness and chaos, and I especially admired their commitment to each other.

I had spent the decade of my late-teens to late-twenties in the trenches of our culture's battle over abortion, and I saw clearly that the crisis of abortion was rooted in another crisis: one of love and family. Is it any wonder that, for many, pregnancy is faced with fear and the temptation to abort when there is no stable, loving marriage, no home to joyfully welcome that new life into?

While I had come to see that we had to awaken the individual to the value of human life in order to end abortion, I also knew that we had to strengthen relationships and families. I hoped for a family of my own to love someday so that, together, we could go out and serve our community, nation, and world. I sensed that for all my activism and advocacy work, creating my own family—if God gave me one—would become the greatest contribution of my life.

In many ways, marriage is under attack today. People see it as an outdated institution. A whole generation of children are jaded by divorce, and many of us question whether joy-filled, lifelong love is even possible. And increasingly, people don't think openness to children in a marriage is important. For some of those who do marry, childless marriage is seen as the sensible choice.

We hear talk of people "falling out of love" or divorcing because "the marriage has run its course." Then there are those who decide to "end their marriage and co-parent," allegedly "out of love and respect for each other." It's all a lie. Love does not divorce. Women and men are complementary. "The two shall become one flesh," said Jesus, citing Genesis. "So they are no longer two, but one flesh" (Matthew 19:5–7 NRSVCE). He says, "What God has joined together, let no one separate" (Mark 10:9), words that are still said in many marriage ceremonies. What is the point of a promise that can be broken or a vow that can be put asunder?

"Love is patient, love is kind," the apostle Paul memorably told the Corinthians. "It does not envy, it does not boast, it is not proud. It does not dishonor others, it is not self-seeking, it is not easily angered, it keeps no record of wrongs. Love does not delight in evil but rejoices with the truth" (1 Corinthians 13:4–6).

Love is relentless. "It always protects, always trusts, always hopes, always perseveres" (v. 7). In sickness and in health, for richer or for poorer. How do we love like that? How do we stay true to a vow to love another flawed human being, when we ourselves struggle with our own flaws, especially in the face of deep wounds, of hurt, or betrayal? With God's love, *only* with God's love. That's the kind of love my soul desired, the love I was made for. Anything less, I knew, was counterfeit.

My parents' marriage of more than thirty-five years was not the result of unfailing chemistry or perfect compatibility. The truth is, for two people, chemistry comes and goes; compatibility ebbs and flows with time. My parents' love was hard-won and weathered. It withstood great personal trial. Polar opposites in temperament and personality, my parents had a marriage that lasted because they *chose* to remain faithful to each other, no matter how difficult it was, and to honor God by honoring their promise to each other. What my parents lived was a sacrament, not only a sacred promise they made to each other and to God but a living witness to the love between Jesus Christ and his church. And with God's help, they kept their promise to love.

I wanted a love like that. Deep down, I think we all do.

As I dated, I looked for a man who had the virtues I wanted to develop myself, such as self-control, humility, and courage. I looked for a man who put God first, a man who was humble and striving to grow, a man who possessed that same rock-solid commitment to the true meaning of marriage: unconditional love and fidelity, no matter what.

One Friday night, I found myself at a fancy lounge crying into a sugary cocktail with my newly engaged childhood best friend, Kaitlyn. I had just moved back to the Bay Area after more than four years in DC. Even though I had dated many guys, I still hadn't found "the one." I was tired of dating and weary of its inevitable heartache, not to mention the considerable time and effort involved. Usually I felt hopeful, but that night I was feeling especially dispirited and lonely.

"Does he even exist?" I asked Kaitlyn despondently, dabbing my eyes with the paper napkin that came with the complimentary bowl of kettle chips. At twenty-eight, I felt ready to find him and hoped to actually *live* the beautiful principles for which I had spent my twenties fighting. Even though intellectually I knew the answer—of course he exists, if that's what God wants for me—I needed to be reminded.

Knowing my struggles all too well, Kait said sympathetically, "It only takes one, Li."

I forced a smile.

"Don't worry," she continued. "God has a plan. And I think he is out there. You just need to meet a guy like my Chris or your brother Joe!"

One week later, we were sitting in an Italian restaurant in Berkeley with Kait's fiancé, as well as my brother Joe and his wife. My brother had invited a sixth person to dinner, who, to confuse things, shared my brother's first name, Joe.

This new Joe and I quickly became friends, best friends. We explored the great hiking trails in Northern California. We shared a love of poetry and music, great literature, travel, and most of all, our faith. We spent time with our friends and families and supported each other through our demanding work. I loved Joe's dry sense of humor, intelligence, wisdom, and intense drive. Whatever we talked about, Joe always had great insight, but his opinions always came with a playfulness and gentleness that put everyone around him at ease.

I have long wrestled with discernment. The words of the wise priest I first met in college, Father Paul, have been especially helpful to me: love starts in our hearts with our feelings and desires but then must move to our "heads" where we weigh the reasons of whether or not to *choose* to love someone. Only when we have made the conscious decision to choose to love can we open up our hearts fully to true love.

There were plenty of reefs and shoals to navigate before we married, but Joe and I shared the same view of marriage. We both believed it was a sacrament that required our total, lifelong fidelity to each other. We saw marriage as requiring an openness to life, a permanent openness. We both hoped to create a family and to be the best father and mother we could be. We saw the great beauty and power in creating a family: families are where faith is first learned, where values are first taught, and where we first learn to love. The family is the basic unit of any functioning society. It's the future of a nation. The effects of one good family can ripple through generations, healing wounds and bringing peace, long after we are gone. Though the challenge was daunting, we wanted to live out our pro-life values through our family, showing the world that there is nothing more beautiful, more wonderful, more mysteriously powerful than the ability to bring new life into the world.

I contemplated Mother Teresa's discovery of her vocation as I thought about this next step in my life. After answering God's call to become a nun, Mother Teresa received a second call from God to go serve the poorest of the poor in Calcutta, India. She called it her "call within a call." For me, my yes to marriage to Joe would be my own "call within a call." I had pursued my cause since I was a teenager. Now my marriage, my family, would be my deeper outpouring to the cause for life.

Maybe you are hoping to get married one day but are unsure of the kind of person you want to marry or when that might happen. Or maybe, because of the models of marriage you have witnessed, you find the prospect of marriage unattractive. It took me years to sort out my own feelings and thoughts about my upbringing and my parents' marriage. None of us can go back in time and change our parents' marriages and how they affected us as children. But all of us, as adults, can learn from the models of marriage to which we've been exposed, the good and the bad, and consciously choose our own path. Here's another Father Paul-ism. He said that as you consider the kind of future and marriage and family you hope for, "Read the book of your childhood. What was good, what was bad, what was missing in it? Write each thing down, and choose to keep the good, heal from the bad, and try to build what was missing!"

Practicing this advice takes work. That work includes understanding the gifts, wounds, and experiences we bring into marriage while also deciding what changes we plan to make to correct our own shortcomings and prepare for what God is calling us to. If done with care, though, that work can help us build a sturdy foundation for the love our hearts are made for.

Finding a spouse who will join you on your own mission is a great gift. Marriage, and the children we might be blessed with, can inspire us to be more courageous, can help us better understand the pains and joys of others, and can expand our own capacity to love. We grow the most in intimate, ordered relationships with others. Not all of us are called to marriage, but for those who do feel called to it, I believe it is worth praying for and preparing for.

The day of our wedding, as my dad walked me down the aisle, I looked ahead into Joe's beaming, handsome face. So many years of questions, heartache, and growth had led to this moment. As we held hands before the altar, I quietly thanked God for entrusting me with this priceless gift. My greatest cause—loving Joe and the family we hoped to create together—had just begun.

CHAPTER 25

Celebrate Life Unconditionally

Caterina was doing better after her stay at the treatment center, but she was still struggling. She had left San Francisco State University and was working as a legal assistant. Now living at home, Cat was often at odds with our parents. In recovery from her eating disorder, she was trying to find new direction for her life. Her aimlessness, smoking, and wanting to stay out late or to sleep over at a new boyfriend's house added to the tension.

For all the inevitable strife, Cat and my parents were trying to make their relationship work. They knew she needed a stable place to live. I tried to spend as much time as I could with her, but I was juggling a busy schedule full of travel, events, and media for Live Action. If that were not enough, I had recently met my future husband, the guy who was not just the average Joe, and he lived ninety minutes away.

One early morning in February at 12:23 a.m, a text from Cat lit up my phone.

Lers, can we get coffee soon?

Of course [I responded quickly]. **When do you want to meet?**

ASAP?

I immediately sensed something major was up. I was going to be busy the next day, but I knew I could move my plans around.

Tmr? I asked.

Yes.

We decided to meet at a coffee shop near her work. As soon as I got there, I could sense her anxiety. We ordered coffee and sandwiches. She picked at her food.

"What is up, Sis?" I asked gently. I wanted to respect her space, but I also wanted her to know how much I cared about whatever she was going through.

"I need you to not tell Mom and Dad or anyone else," she began nervously, "but I missed my period."

"Oh, wow," I said, less in surprise than in concern. "Did you take a pregnancy test yet?"

"No." I saw the fear on her face. I reached over and hugged her.

"Listen, Sis, we are going to figure this out. I am here to support you 100 percent," I reassured her. "If you are pregnant, I've got your back."

"Thanks, Lers," Cat said. Her gratitude was real.

"Would the baby be with Allan?" I asked.

She nodded.

Allan was a new boyfriend, a guy she had met through one of our brothers. Cat had just started seeing him about two months before. I hadn't met him yet, but I knew he and Cat had quickly become friends. Two adrenaline junkies, they both loved driving fast on mountain roads and climbing cliffs on the California coast. The fact that she had, at least on occasion, stayed overnight at his apartment prompted some of the fights between her and our parents.

"Do you want to go take a pregnancy test together, Sis?" I asked. I wanted to protect her, support her, and, if she were pregnant, to protect her baby. Cat had struggled a lot, and I didn't yet know enough about Allan to trust him.

"Sure, let's do it," she said.

We got into my car and headed to CVS. Caterina picked the most accurate pregnancy test we could find, a two-pack called Early Detection.

"Let's just do it in the bathroom here," she said.

I agreed. There was no better place to go close by, and our parents' house, even if it had been close, was exactly the wrong place for something this sensitive. I bought the test kit, and we got the CVS bathroom key. The single-stall bathroom was cleaner than what you might find at a gas station, but not by much. We had to laugh. It was so *not* the place a woman wants to learn she is about to be a first-time mom.

"Ready?" I said. We both smiled nervously. Cat opened the box and took out the instructions. I told her she could just go ahead and pee on the stick, but she wanted to read every word. Then she took the test. We stood breathlessly, watching the stick slowly reveal two faint pink lines.

"I'm pregnant," she whispered.

"Oh, Sis! I am so happy. Congratulations! I can't believe it!" I said, tears welling up in my eyes. She looked one part surprised, one part terrified, one part elated.

"Wow. Okay. Thank you. I'm pregnant."

"Sis, I am here to support you 100 percent," I repeated. "Whatever you need. I know our family is going to support you and this baby."

We left CVS, and Cat asked me to drop her off at work. She joked about needing to give up cigarettes. I told her confidently I knew she could do it, and that this baby would help her be healthier than ever.

Driving away, I felt a pang of anxiety. I knew Cat was pro-life. I knew she could be brave, but I also knew that earlier in her life she had lived in some dark spaces emotionally. The Caterina I knew would not even consider abortion, but I could not suppress my fears. Allan did not share our background or all of our values. I had no way of knowing whether he would support Cat's choice of life.

Thousands of questions loomed about how my baby sister would grow into the role of a mother or, if she chose instead, how she would navigate the adoption process. Despite my concerns, I felt a strong sense of peace. This baby was not an accident but a gift from God. I sensed that this little life would help Cat turn her life around, awakening in my sister the powerful love and bravery deep inside her. She had shown the courage to accept healing for the sake of her own life. I had witnessed that. Now, I prayed for something more: the privilege of witnessing my sister's powerful yes to her child's life.

After dropping Cat off at work, I headed over to my parents' house. I wanted to be there when Cat got home. My mom was out of town visiting our grandparents in Tennessee, but my Dad and my sister Nina were home. Neither suspected anything when I came over; I often dropped in to visit and spend the night. Throughout the rest of the day, Caterina and I continued to text. I can be here if you want to tell Dad or FaceTime Mom and tell her, I told her. But no rush or pressure. Whenever you feel ready. I knew she needed their support, and as difficult as I knew the news that their nineteen-year-old daughter was pregnant would be, I knew they would do everything they could to help her.

Later that night, Caterina and I sat at our parents' kitchen table talking quietly about her pregnancy. My dad was upstairs in his study, reading.

"I'm just terrified about what they will say," Cat said to me. "They will be so disappointed. Maybe they will kick me out. I have no idea how I'm gonna do this."

"They won't kick you out, Sis," I assured her. I could only imagine what she was feeling. I had talked to a lot of girls in similar positions over the years. I had seen how overwhelming the fear could be. "Look, I know Mom and Dad don't approve of sex outside of marriage, but they'll love this baby."

Over the years, I've come to reflect a lot on the whole concept of unexpected pregnancy. I think that our society has set up whole generations of young women and men for failure in this regard.

We tell young people that sex outside of marriage is normal and even healthy, as long as no children are conceived or diseases contracted. "Just make sure you don't get pregnant!" is the common advice. We are told to practice "safe sex" to avoid creating a new life. But I think this view of sex and children is totally backward. It is sex outside of marriage that is wrong, not bringing new children into the world.

In sex without marriage, two people give each other their bodies in the most intimate way but haven't promised each other their love, their commitment, and their fidelity. Sex without marriage is ultimately a lie that we tell with our bodies. We give ourselves physically to each other, but we don't give the promise of lifelong love. And because sex is designed to bring children into the world, sex without marriage is even more harmful, because two people who aren't committed to each other, and who never intended to be parents in the first place, will struggle to embrace a child they may conceive.

But a new child's life is *always* good. A new life is always worth celebrating, no matter how he or she came into existence. Your value and my value are not dependent on the intentions of our parents. While I knew my parents would not approve of Caterina sleeping with Allan, I couldn't imagine that they wouldn't embrace this new life.

Most of my family are night owls, and Caterina and I continued to talk late into the night while my dad stayed awake upstairs with his books. Finally, Cat stood up and said anxiously, "Okay, I am just going to tell him. Let's just do it."

We both marched upstairs and opened the study door. Our dad was in his recliner, his nose in a book. "Dad," Caterina walked right up to him. "Dad . . ." she continued hesitantly. "I have something to tell you."

My dad put the book down. "Of course, what is it, my daughter?"

"Dad, I'm pregnant."

His eyes widened, realization hitting him. There was a moment of quiet. Then he started to reassure her. I watched as the tension on her face melted away. My dad spent the next thirty minutes affirming her and her baby, telling her that he loved her in his own gentle and philosophical way. He talked to her about responsibility, and the fact that her life would change forever but that it didn't mean her life was over. Instead, her life had taken a new direction and that beautiful things were going to happen.

After a little while, as the conversation slowed down, my dad said, "Now we need to celebrate!" He left the study for a minute and came back, holding three cups in one hand and a bottle of champagne in another. "I'm a granddad again," he said, grinning. He popped the bottle and began pouring glasses. "Dad," Cat protested, "I can't drink! I'm pregnant!" My dad and I cheered for her instead.

He sat back down next to Cat and said to her, "I know you know I am disappointed in how this happened, and I wish it hadn't happened under these circumstances. But I am so excited to meet my grandchild. And I am so proud of you."

Over the next several months, Caterina wrestled with whether or not to place her baby boy for an adoption. Our family told her we would support her in whatever she decided, and each of us wrestled with our own doubts and fears about how Caterina would become a mother, or how she would feel placing her son for adoption. There was no easy answer. I spent hours with Caterina scrolling through adoption websites that featured countless families hoping to adopt. But ultimately, Caterina chose to parent. Her little boy, with his bright blue eyes just like hers and his huge smile just like his dad's, would bring more joy to our lives than we could imagine. Every day with him is a celebration.

The abortion lobby says that an unplanned pregnancy is something to escape from: that a young mother is better off, at least most of the time, choosing to end the life of her child. But saying yes to life and embracing the struggle, despite the challenges that come with it, opens up horizons of joy and meaning that would never have been possible before. Children are intrinsically valuable, and they deserve our love and respect. Pregnancy, labor and delivery, and raising a child, all require sacrifice. It is rarely easy. But if we reject the struggle or encourage others to, thinking we will be better off, we run from opportunities to love. Beyond the moral wrong we commit, we are rejecting a gift. We are rejecting joy.

Life is full of the unexpected. No matter what circumstance we face, even if it seems like a great obstacle or a difficulty, the unexpected can be transformed into a blessing—if we choose to allow it. Caterina lived that. She said yes to life and embraced it, even when she didn't feel ready or strong. She chose celebration. She chose to love her baby unconditionally. It changed her life—and all our lives—for the better. "It's amazing how your perspective changes when someone else is depending on you," Caterina told me in the weeks leading up to her baby's birth. "Everything I do I want to do for this baby. I want to be healthier, stronger, better, for him."

Life is always worth celebrating: the gift of our lives, the gift of our loved ones' lives, the gift of the lives of the people we fight for and even the people who oppose us. It can be easy to forget this. Maybe in the cause you are fighting for you see so much injustice and heartache, you struggle to see the joy. In the midst of the heavy darkness, it can be hard to experience the light. But silver linings are there if we're willing to open our eyes and see them.

I believe that life is one long lesson in celebration coexisting with grief. I know that my own struggles and hurts over the years have taught me more about love and strength than I would have known otherwise. In this sense, even our wounds are worth celebrating. They prove that we are alive, that we are still fighting, that we have the power to love. Being a force for change in a wounded world requires celebration, especially when the hard moments threaten to eclipse the joy that is at the heart of life. Being a force for change requires a radical affirmation of all that is good and true. And it requires that we step back from the battle and marvel at the beauty.

There's a reason one day a week is set aside as a day of rest in the Abrahamic faiths. As a part of that rest, it is a day to marvel at the good works done during the rest of the week, which is what God Himself did when He created the world, according to the account in Genesis. It is a day for leisure and prayer, no matter the trials or struggles of the week before. Christians set aside Sunday for rest as a way to honor and worship God—to worship the Power and Person behind all that is good and beautiful and true in the world. Our lives must be punctuated by intentional and unconditional celebration of the good, of remembering and cherishing all we are fighting for.

What do you have to celebrate? What is the good news you can cherish, the beauty and goodness you can enjoy—in your life or the lives of others? What are the wins, even if they seem small in the larger scheme of your work, that you can rejoice over as you fight for your cause?

Live Action gets messages and comments every day from people who say they've been inspired by our work, but the notes that make us all pause from the daily grind and celebrate are the ones from young women like Veronica.

Unexpectedly pregnant at sixteen, Veronica considered all her options and went to Planned Parenthood. They confirmed her pregnancy and then tried to sell her on an abortion. Unsure of what to do, Veronica went home and did a YouTube search for "What is an abortion?" It led her to one of Live Action's Abortion Procedures videos. In tears, Veronica decided right then that she could not allow what she had seen on that video to be done to her baby. A fierce protectiveness rose up within her, and she decided to fight for the life of the child within her. She would eventually give birth to a little boy, whom she named Myles. Veronica would contact us and share her story, sending us a picture of her beautiful baby son.

Our whole team lights up when we get incredible messages like the one from Veronica. It is a supreme joy to discover that our work helped save a life. We know that we are not only helping spare a baby from the violence of an abortion, but that we are helping to inspire his mother to embrace him and reject an act that would devastate her too. It's cause for immediate celebration. We keep a running database file of all the good news we hear—hearts inspired, minds changed, lives saved. It is our running celebration list.

The images of these little ones and their brave mothers are the banners we carry in our hearts, brimming with joy, as we march forward to fight for life.

CHAPTER 26

Beware of False Compassion

Newly married, Joe and I had just moved to Los Angeles and discovered within weeks that we were pregnant. We were thrilled, and I immediately started hunting for an OB/GYN. I was hoping to find an OB who was pro-life. I asked around for weeks but was having trouble getting referrals. While most doctors won't do what are considered elective abortions, and certainly won't work at an abortion clinic, many may commit abortions if the baby is sick or disabled.

A friend recommended a doctor who did not do abortions. Encouraged by the news, I made an appointment. On the scheduled day, I headed to her office in one of the nicer parts of Los Angeles. The clinic had valet parking. When I handed over the keys to my badly-in-need-of-a-wash, cluttered Hyundai Elantra with cloth seats to the parking attendant, I felt more than a little bit out of place—I always felt that way in posh parts of Los Angeles. The office was pristine. Several women sat in the waiting room, fashionably dressed, with designer handbags and shoes.

After an ultrasound and check-in with a friendly nurse, I sat down with the doctor in her office. She was kind and professional, and I immediately felt some relief. Perhaps I had finally found my doctor! After a few minutes of chitchat and a discussion of my pregnancy, I mentioned that she had been referred to me as a pro-life doctor who did not do abortions. I explained why that fact was important to me.

"Correct." She nodded. "I don't do any terminations, any elective terminations."

Elective terminations. Those words typically mean an abortion without the rationale of a health defect in the baby to justify the abortion. For too many doctors, the proper medical response to a sick or disabled baby is abortion. My heart sank. *Oh no.* Why did she use the word *elective*?

I asked her hesitantly, "So, do you do any terminations that aren't elective?"

The doctor grew visibly uncomfortable. "Well, I won't do any terminations if the baby has Down Syndrome or anything like that. I'm a pastor's daughter. I'm really conservative. Almost all the other doctors here do those abortions. But I sleep well at night. There's only one other doctor here as conservative as I am. She's an Orthodox Jew, but even she will do a Down Syndrome abortion."

Down Syndrome abortion? She was talking about her colleague dismembering and killing a baby with Down Syndrome for no other reason than the baby had Down Syndrome. She said this without a hint of outrage. The tension in the office was thick. I felt her obvious discomfort, and I shared it. How strange that we have to have these conversations in a doctor's office. I was there hoping to find a doctor to care for me and my preborn child, yet here we were, discussing which class of babies can be killed and by whom.

I hated having to ask the follow-up question, but I sensed there was more to the story than what she had shared.

"It's really good you don't abort babies with Down Syndrome," I said slowly. "I'm glad to hear that. I am also very conservative. I am Catholic. To clarify, you don't do any abortions at all, or you do some, just in certain cases?"

"I do some. But only if the baby is going to die," she answered a little flatly.

"What do you mean by 'if the baby is going to die'?" I asked.

"They are anencephaly cases," she said.

I was very familiar with such cases. Live Action News has done considerable reporting on the syndrome. These babies develop in the womb with most of their brain missing. Sometimes, only the brain stem is present. Many end up being miscarried. Others do not survive birth or live only for the first few hours thereafter. In some cases, however, these babies can live for years. There was a beautiful story Live Action featured of a baby boy named Jaxon. Jaxon had anencephaly, and the doctors told his parents he would die and recommended abortion several times. The parents refused, knowing that his life had value even though he was disabled. Even if his life promised to be very short, it was not their right—or anyone's right—to deprive him of it. Jaxon ended up living five years. And although his doctors said it would be physically impossible for him to speak, Jaxon learned to say "Mama," and "Dada," a miracle given how much of his brain was missing.

I realized that my would-be doctor was willing to kill a baby like Jaxon.

"We all die," I said quietly. I looked at her, and she looked back at me. Inside, I was so full of sadness.

"I work with a group that does considerable reporting on these cases," I said. "I know a lot of these babies die before birth, but some live longer, even for a few years. And they bring a lot of joy to their families."

"I don't think that's possible," she said stiffly. This doctor, like most, did not like thinking about what she was capable of doing. I could tell she considered herself the most morally conscious doctor in her practice, maybe even in all of Los Angeles. I had inadvertently trespassed on a part of her conscience that had grown numb.

I pulled up Jaxon's story on my phone and offered to show it to her. The doctor glanced at it but was still in disbelief. Usually not at a loss for words, I fell momentarily quiet.

"Even if babies die in a miscarriage, or at birth, isn't that different than a doctor ending their life?" I finally asked. "If there was a born child who lost most of their brain function in a tragic accident, but wasn't on life support, would it be okay to intentionally kill them?"

She paused. I could tell the conversation felt overwhelming to her. It certainly overwhelmed me. It felt like the room was spinning and time was in suspension.

"It's something I do," she said defensively. "But I won't do most abortions. I was even offered a partnership at a big firm here, and I said no because they wanted me to do elective. I won't do abortions if there's a physical disability, even a bad one."

The doctor explained that she almost hadn't gone into obstetrics and gynecology because there are so many troubling ethical issues. She cited assisted reproductive technology (ART), genetic selection, and the implantation of multiple babies with the expectation of aborting some.

"I couldn't do any of that," she said.

I looked at her silently. I sensed that she felt justified in her refusal to do *most* abortions. She felt she was the moral one, even while she killed the babies with anencephaly. Her moral worldview contradicted itself, and it seemed she had never reflected on the incoherence of it all.

"Is it a problem?" she then asked me quietly. "I mean, is it an issue for you?"

She wasn't confrontational, and neither was I. I felt so badly for her. I felt so badly for the babies. I was at a loss for words.

"Thank you for being so up front with me," I said. "I don't know. Do you know any doctors who won't do any terminations at all?"

"No." She sighed. "I'm the most conservative doctor I know."

"I understand," I said. We looked at each other, the tension high. But more than that, a sadness permeated the room.

"I will be in touch," I said.

At that moment, I did not know if I could work with her. I wasn't sure if I should go see another doctor. More than anything, though, I felt like going somewhere and crying. The doctor seemed as shaken as I was.

Leaving the office, I felt torn inside. The awkwardness, the vulnerability of being there pregnant, her pain, but most of all, shock. I knew I shouldn't be shocked. Abortion was everywhere. But here was a doctor, saying how she was a Christian, a pastor's daughter, the most conservative of all the doctors she knew, who said she was against abortions, and yet she killed babies with anencephaly—and didn't even consider it killing.

Tears flowed as soon as I got into the car. I couldn't stop crying. Big, deep sobs. In working with Live Action over the years, I've seen and heard the worst stories. I have had many opportunities to grieve, to cry. But this time, the grief felt primal. I had my own baby in my womb, a little life with his heart beating, arms and legs kicking. And the doctor I hoped would deliver my baby was the same doctor who tore into pieces living babies with disabilities. These little anencephaly babies were being killed in the name of compassion—a false compassion. They weren't given the chance to be held in the arms of their mothers, even if only for a few moments. It was as if their own mothers, their own fathers, wished they had never even existed. They were destroyed before they had taken their first breath or opened their eyes.

Resolve welled up inside me, the same resolve I had felt since I was a teenager, but even stronger, building like a current that breaks through a dam. Anger, heartache, and determination—all in one. I was a mother now. I *knew* what it was like to be a mother, to have a child in my womb who desperately needed safety and love. How could we continue to allow this cruelty? How could we turn our own wombs into death chambers for our children? I called Joe and told him I'd met with the doctor.

"She does abortions too," I said, still crying, "on babies with anencephaly. It is so sad. It is so sad. Is there anyone in L.A. who doesn't? The medical system is so bad."

"I am so sorry, love. It is so sad," he consoled me. "We will find another doctor."

Abortion taints much of today's medical profession. It is increasingly full of practitioners who at some point were told that abortion should be accepted as a normal part of healthcare. Over the years, I've corresponded with medical students distressed because they have been told they must watch or commit abortions as part of their medical training. (They have legal rights to decline, and so I often find myself connecting them with legal counsel.)

Increasingly prevalent is the justification that abortion is medically necessary, and therefore, it should be legal. Abortion proponents argue either that the baby is disabled and therefore should be aborted or that the mother's health or life is at risk and, therefore, her pregnancy must be terminated. Sadly, this ideology is considered the norm by most doctors. It is driven by a false sense of compassion—that by supporting abortion for these reasons, they are doing the loving thing.

But the truth is that abortion is never medically necessary, and it is never loving to kill. Some 4,500 pro-life American OB/GYNs hold that it is possible to care for both a mother and her preborn child, even in high risk situations, without intentionally ending the life of the child.[1] A mother in need may be given medical treatments, such as chemotherapy for example, that may have an adverse effect on her developing child, but that is not an abortion.

In extreme and rare cases when pregnancy complications threaten a mother's life, such as toxemia or preeclampsia, the doctor may need to deliver the child prematurely, attempting to save the lives of both the child and the mother. But this is not an abortion. The doctor's intent is not to kill the baby. An abortion is different: it is designed to produce a dead baby, and it targets the baby's body for destruction. Pre-term delivery is much safer than late-term abortion. Keep in mind that in every abortion, the baby still must be delivered. Killing that child before birth or during delivery does nothing to improve the mother's health.

In an opinion piece I coauthored with Dr. Donna Harrison, we put it this way: "The reality is that even if the baby cannot live after we separate mother and baby, there is an undeniable difference between a doctor trying to save the baby after that separation against long odds, and an abortionist deliberately and intentionally killing the baby within the womb."[2]

As we explained in the article, in a late-term abortion, the doctor injects the baby with a poison to stop the baby's heart. Labor is then induced, which takes between two and four days. "Abortion is not a procedure done in true emergency situations," we concluded. "The purpose of an abortion is to produce a dead baby, not to separate the mother and the baby."

False compassion, the rationalization used to justify these abortions, is prevalent today. Just as I did in the doctor's office, you may find it in places you least expect it. Our discernment in recognizing it is essential. The word *compassion* literally means to "suffer with." But false compassion refuses to suffer with; instead, in the name of mercy, it often advocates to end the life of the one who suffers. That isn't solidarity with those who hurt; it's the ultimate rejection of an ongoing relationship with those who hurt. False compassion offers an immoral solution to a problem, real or perceived, in the name of mercy.

Twisted compassion is more dangerous than outright malice because it is more difficult to detect. Because of all the brokenness and pain in this world, we are sometimes told that it is compassionate to kill, that death is better than life, that abandoning our responsibility is better than accepting it. But it is simply not our right to take an innocent human life, no matter how much suffering we think we or another may face.

We must do our best to alleviate suffering, but never by eliminating the sufferer. We do not advocate for sexually trafficked survivors by calling for their deaths. We don't work to protect the elderly, the frail, the poor, or the disenfranchised by saying it would be better to end their lives. Imagine how ridiculous it would have been if abolitionists had called for the killing of slaves to spare them the pain of their enslavement. If we love someone, we don't wish that they die. We should always fight to save lives and to make life better, not to end lives.

There may come a limit to our ability to stop our own or someone else's suffering, and that's when we can remember that it is possible for suffering to be redemptive. We shouldn't run from it blindly. In many situations, we voluntarily choose to suffer to achieve something good. It is our love of control and love of self that tempts us to run from suffering. When considering an abortion, false compassion suggests abortion is the answer to the suffering of a terminally ill or disabled baby. However, in these cases I've discovered that the reason for the abortion is often more about the parents' inability to bear the thought of having a disabled child than it is concern for the sick child's suffering. Like Jaxon, those who suffer or have severe disability can experience great love and joy—but only if those around them are willing to protect their right to live and to offer them that love.

We should embrace the suffering of others and do our best to help them in their pain while affirming the gift of their life. This will require sacrifice, but when we will the good of the other, even to the point of pain, we discover the real richness of love.

CHAPTER 27

Begin Anew

How do we restore justice when so much injustice has been done? Since the 1973 *Roe v. Wade* decision, it is estimated that more than sixty million children have been killed in the United States by abortion. The global number since 1980 is estimated to exceed 1.5 billion.[1] But no matter how much of this evil we expose, my work has shown me again and again that our politics will not change until our people change.

Live Action today focuses on changing the culture, one person at a time, by sharing truth that transforms lives. Only awakened hearts and minds can change the world.

We recognize that abortion is a sign of a rotting culture. Many other things have gone wrong to get us to a place where killing babies has become an accepted practice. And the best place to start fixing these wrongs is in the family.

Homes and families are where the future is formed. In the love between a man and a woman, and through the creative power of God, new human lives enter the world. A family is where children learn their worth, learn how to love, learn how to live. It's why the health of a family directly shapes the health of a nation. The family is where God's eternal purposes come to life; it is the beginning of each human story, a love story whose ends are in eternity.

Starting a family doesn't mean we leave the fight. It means we dare to rebuild our nation, even on a battlefield. I believe that in a world so often restless and cynical, saying yes to romance, to love, to the everyday tasks of marriage and family is its own quiet revolution. Defying the forces of evil, one man and one woman making a little home where vulnerability, tenderness, and laughter can thrive is a subversive act. It also means creating a family is the supreme act of defiance—a celebration of life in the midst of war.

In the last week of 2019, after twenty-four hours of labor, I gave birth to my son, Peter. Labor was the most painful, intense, and raw experience of my life, but one I would endure a thousand times over for Peter.

My life was coming full circle. In the midst of labor, I heard a voice by the delivery room door. It was Caterina's. She was peering around the privacy curtain.

"Hi, Cat," I said weakly. "I'm about to have another contraction, hold on a second."

I breathed through the wave of intensity that consumed my body. As it subsided, I turned to Caterina, who was now next to me. In the months leading up to this moment, she had coached me and encouraged me, transmitting the lessons she had learned from her own pregnancy and labor to bring her son into the world. She gently put her hand on my back. My hair was falling into my face, sweat pouring over me.

"Can you French braid my hair?" I asked.

"Of course, Sis." She smiled as she ran her fingers through my hair. We sat there together for the next hour, me breathing through contractions. The gift of her presence consoled me until my mother arrived after taking an early morning flight. Six months before, Caterina had married her best friend, Allan, and now was pregnant with their second baby. Cat had found the secret.

It is wild to experience the love I have for Peter, the innate protectiveness and willingness to do whatever I have to for him, no matter how difficult or painful. Looking at his sweet face, his little body nestled in my arms, I marvel at the pure gift of his life. Now that he is here in all his wonder, I can't imagine the world without him.

Being a mother brings the pain of this fight for life even more intensely to my heart. I can't help but think of the babies killed by abortion. I can't help but imagine again the terrible pain that a woman who has had an abortion must feel once she sees for the first time what that abortion really does. But her pain and heartache can bring good. Heartache shows us a problem that needs fixing, a wound that needs healing, and a cause that needs joining.

What is the vision for which we fight?

We fight for the innocence of all children and their right to be loved and protected. We fight for the sacredness of every human being from the first moment of their existence, when God himself designs a new, unique, and totally irreplaceable life. We fight for justice, for the day when our laws treat all people equally and no one is left out. We fight for that break-through moment when respect for God's justice reigns in every human heart. We fight for the dignity of every woman and girl, that each one might know her worth. We fight for motherhood and fatherhood and for the sacredness of family. We fight for life, for the precious gift of a life lived as fully and abundantly as God intended here on earth and in hope of the eternity to come.

This fight needs men and women of courage and conviction, of every background, of all ages.

The fight needs those who once cooperated with injustice but now bravely witness against it.

The fight needs the girl who doesn't think she has much to offer because she's too young and too inexperienced.

The fight needs the student whose workload cannot suppress their passion to repair the brokenness of the world they study.

The fight needs the creatives, the artists, the scientists, the medical workers, the service workers, the administrators, the lawyers, the teachers, and the business leaders who pour themselves into their professions every day but still see the crisis and refuse to be silent.

The fight needs the mothers and fathers, busy with their children, who grieve for other children who will be deprived of love.

The fight needs all of us, no matter our wounds or mistakes or imperfections.

We fight with confidence, knowing that God's mercy and justice will prevail. Together we can rebuild the broken foundations, restore what has been devastated, and renew our wounded world (Isaiah 61:4).

Together we can celebrate the new beginning. We can even close our eyes and allow ourselves to dream.

Acknowledgments

To God, my heavenly Father, Savior, and comfort, for giving me everything I have, all that I am, and the promise of eternity with you.

To my Joe, thank you for being my husband, my best friend, my most trusted advisor, my biggest fan, my wisest critic, and my all-around rock. I love you.

To Peter, the littlest love of my life, how did I get so blessed to be your mother? Thank you for letting me finish this book while I was entrusted with the precious first months of your life.

To my mother, you've poured heart and soul into raising me and us kids and your unending sacrifice, advice, cheerleading, and unconditional support not only made this book possible but the entire story it tells. Thank you for your unconditional love.

To my father, thank you for being the consummate Renaissance man, my favorite editor and thought-partner, the one who set the standard high for my own future husband, and the one who taught me to love the good, the true, the beautiful.

To my brothers, to Nina and to Cat, thank you for letting me include you in this book and being some of my best friends and biggest inspirations. I love you.

To my Live Action Team, thank you so much for doing the heavy lifting in our fight for life. You are each brilliant, talented, loving, and brave. Thanks for making me proud and inspiring me.

To Kaitlyn, thank you for being my (other) best friend, understanding my heart and life in ways I do not even, and being my expert editor.

To my dear grandparents, Grandma Judy, Grandpa Don, Grandpa Rose, Grandpa Joe, Grandma Carmella. Thank you for your unconditional love and encouragement since I was a little girl. I love you more than words can express.

To my amazing in-laws, thank you so much for the incredible job you did on the study guide for this book and for all your amazing support. I am so grateful to be part of your family.

To my elementary literature and poetry teachers Mrs. Cherniss and Mrs. Silva. Thank you for helping spark my childhood dream of being an author and for nurturing the future writer in me. Thank you for being my favorite childhood teachers.

To each and every person who has supported our mission, some of you from the very beginning, with your money, your time, and your courage. Thank you for investing in Live Action and our movement to save lives.

Jack, thank you for being an expert hand to help me wrestle this manuscript to completion. You are a Yoda.

Alex, thank you for believing in this book and me as an author from day #1 and making the whole adventure possible.

Jessica, thank you for challenging me and drawing out of me the best book possible. To the whole publishing team at Nelson, thank you for your patience, warmth, and skill.

A special thank you to the wisdom, friendship, and support of Laura Brasov, Pat Lencioni, Larry Simpson, Jonathan Terrell, Chris Mundwiller, Tessa Rogers, Claire Komives, Carole Decosse, Sue Ellen Browder, Father Anthony Sortino, Father Paul Donlan, Father Marcel Guarnizo, Jenny Guarnizo, Cristina Barba Whalen, Stephanie Gray Connors, Bernadette Peters, Liz Connors, the Bengards, the Smiths, Jen Fulwiler, and Robert and Molly Rose.

And big shout-out to the talented Danielle Lussier Six and Joe Kim for helping bring the creative vision of the cover to life.

Notes

Dare to Fight for a Better World

1. Aleksandr I. Solzhenitsyn, *The Gulag Archipelago, Volume 1: An Experiment in Literary Investigation* (New York: HarperCollins, 1985, 2007), 312.

Chapter 1: Let Your Heart Break

1. Alison Mitchell, "Clinton, in Emotional Terms, Explains His Abortion Veto," *New York Times*, December 14, 1996, https://www.nytimes.com/1996/12/14 /us/clinton-in-emotional-terms-explains-his-abortion-veto.html.
2. Melissa Healy, "Clinton Vetoes Ban on Procedure in Late Abortions," *Los Angeles Times*, April 11, 1996, https://www.latimes.com/archives/la-xpm -1996-04-11-mn-57381-story.html.

Chapter 2: Find Your Heroes

1. Corrie ten Boom, *The Hiding Place* (Peabody, MA: Hendrickson Publishers, 1971, 2006), 262.
2. Ten Boom, *The Hiding Place*, 240.
3. "Biography of Saint Maximilian Kolbe," Saint Maximilian Kolbe Church, accessed October 8, 2020, https://www.stmaximiliankolbechurch.com /about-us/biography-of-saint-maximilian.
4. C. S. Lewis Institute, "On the Reading of Old Books," *Reflections* (February 2010), https://www.cslewisinstitute.org/On_Reading_Old_Books.
5. Mother Teresa, "National Prayer Breakfast Address," American Rhetoric, February 3, 1994, https://www.americanrhetoric.com/speeches/mother teresanationalprayerbreakfast.htm.
6. Mother Teresa, "National Prayer Breakfast Address."

Chapter 4: Know Your Worth

1. Viktor E. Frankl, *Man's Search for Meaning* (New York: Pocket Books, 1959, 1992), 87–88.
2. Josef Pieper, *Josef Pieper: An Anthology* (San Francisco: Ignatius Press, 1989), 28.
3. Thomas Aquinas, quoted in Joshua Schipper, "To Love Is to Will the Good of the Other," *Today's Catholic*, October 25, 2018, https://today scatholic.org/to-love-is-to-will-the-good-of-the-other/.

Chapter 5: Let God Find You

1. Francis Thompson, "The Hound of Heaven," public domain, https://www .ewtn.com/catholicism/library/hound-of-heaven-4117.

Chapter 6: Find Your Cause

1. Hannah Arendt, *Eichmann in Jerusalem: A Report on the Banality of Evil* (New York: Penguin Books, 2006).
2. "Abortion Statistics: United States Data and Trends," National Right to Life Educational Foundation, 2017, https://nrlc.org/uploads/factsheets /FS01AbortionintheUS.pdf.
3. On a recent annual report, Planned Parenthood states, "Approximately 393,000 unintended pregnancies [were] averted by Planned Parenthood contraceptive services," which is approximately 1,076 abortions a day over the course of a year. Planned Parenthood, *Annual Report 2018–2019*, (New York, 2019), 7, https://www.plannedparenthood.org/uploads/filer_public /2e/da/2eda3f50-82aa-4ddb-acce-c2854c4ea80b/2018-2019_annual _report.pdf.
4. Margaret Sanger, *Woman and the New Race* (New York: Truth Publishing, 1920), 68.
5. Lawrence B. Finer and Stanley K. Henshaw, "Estimates of U.S. Abortion Incidence in 2001 and 2002," Guttmacher Institute, May 2005, https://www .guttmacher.org/sites/default/files/pdfs/pubs/2005/05/18/ab_incidence.pdf.
6. "Worldwide Abortion Statistics," Abort73.com, October 10, 2018, https:// abort73.com/abortion_facts/worldwide_abortion_statistics/.
7. Mother Teresa, "National Prayer Breakfast Address," American Rhetoric, February 3, 1994, https://www.americanrhetoric.com/speeches/mother teresanationalprayerbreakfast.htm.
8. "BUCK v. BELL, Superintendent of State Colony Epileptics and Feeble

Minded," Legal Information Institute, accessed October 10, 2020, https://www.law.cornell.edu/supremecourt/text/274/200.

9. Margaret Sanger, *The Autobiography of Margaret Sanger* (Mineola, NY: Dover Publications, 1938, 1971, 2004), 39.

10. Margaret Sanger, *The Pivot of Civilization* (Washington, DC: Scott-Townsend Publishers, 1975), 89.

11. "Number of Births, Population Prevalence of Down Syndrome Estimated in Nine States," Science Daily, August 28, 2017, https://www.sciencedaily .com/releases/2017/08/170828143554.htm.

Chapter 7: Just Start

1. Rachel K. Jones, Jacqueline E. Darroch, and Stanley K. Henshaw, "Patterns in the Socioeconomic Characteristics of Women Obtaining Abortions in 2000–2001," *Perspectives on Sexual and Reproductive Health* 34, no. 5 (September/October 2002), https://www.guttmacher.org/journals/psrh /2002/09/patterns-socioeconomic-characteristics-women-obtaining -abortions-2000-2001.

2. "The Case for Life," Life Training Institute, https://prolifetraining.com /resources/the-case-for-life/.

Chapter 8: Prepare to Stand Alone

1. *Joan of Arc in Her Own Words*, compiled and translated by William Trask (Brooklyn: Turtle Point Press, 1996), 11.

Chapter 9: Leave Your Comfort Zone

1. In 2004, women aged eighteen to nineteen accounted for 10.5 percent of all abortions, and women between the ages of twenty and twenty-four accounted for 33.2 percent of all abortions, for a total of 44 percent within the eighteen to twenty-four age range. Stanley K. Henshaw and Kathryn Kost, "Trends in the Characteristics of Women Obtaining Abortions, 1974–2004," Guttmacher Institute, August 2008, https://www.guttmacher.org/report/trends- characteristics-women-obtaining-abortions-1974-2004-supplemental-tables#.

2. "About Planned Parenthood Generation Action," Planned Parenthood, accessed October 11, 2020, https://www.plannedparenthoodaction.org /communities/planned-parenthood-generation-action/about-planned -parenthood-generation-action.

3. The state of Florida recently updated its abortion reporting system and therefore has some of the best data available about the reasons women cite for having an abortion. According to the Charlotte Lozier Institute, "Florida sorts reasons for abortions into eight general categories: life of the mother; physical health of the mother; emotional or psychological health of the mother; abnormality in the baby; rape; incest; social or economic concerns; and elective. . . . In 2018, elective abortions made up . . . 75 percent of all abortions in Florida." Tessa Longbons, "Abortion Reporting: Florida (2018)," Charlotte Lozier Institute, April 29, 2019, https://lozierinstitute.org/abortion-reporting-florida-2018/.

4. "About Half of U.S. Abortion Patients Report Using Contraception in the Month They Became Pregnant," Guttmacher Institute, January 11, 2018, https://www.guttmacher.org/news-release/2018/about-half-us-abortion -patients-report-using-contraception-month-they-became.

5. Jeyling Chou, "[A Closer Look] Ashe Center Offers Pregnancy Counseling, Services," *Daily Bruin*, January 25, 2005, https://dailybruin.com/2005/01 /25/a-closer-look-ashe-center-offe.

Chapter 10: Build a Team

1. Sun Tzu, "Five Essentials for Victory" in *The Art of War* (Minneapolis: Filiquarian Publishing, 2006), 15.

2. Derek Sivers, "How to Start a Movement," TED2010, February 2010, https:// www.ted.com/talks/derek_sivers_how_to_start_a_movement?language=en.

Chapter 11: Expose the Evil

1. Saul Friedländer, *Nazi Germany and the Jews, Volume 1: The Years of Persecution 1933–1939* (London: Phoenix Books, 1997), 6.

2. Gregg Cunningham, "Guest Blog: Gregg Cunningham's Reply to Simcha Fisher's Demand That the Pro-Life Movement Cover Up the Horrors of Abortion," American Freedom Law Center (blog), January 28, 2013, https://www.americanfreedomlawcenter.org/2013/01/28/guest-article -gregg-cunningham/.

3. Jonathan Klein, "Photos That Changed the World," TED2010, February 2010, https://www.ted.com/talks/jonathan_klein_photos_that_changed _the_world?language=en.

4. "Abortion Statistics in the United States," Wikipedia, last edited

December 16, 2020, https://en.wikipedia.org/wiki/Abortion_statistics_in
_the_United_States.

5. David Livingstone Smith, "'Less Than Human': The Psychology of Cruelty,"
Talk of the Nation, NPR, March 29, 2011, https://www.npr.org/2011
/03/29/134956180/criminals-see-their-victims-as-less-than-human.

6. David Livingstone Smith, *Less Than Human: Why We Demean, Enslave,
and Exterminate Others* (New York: St. Martin's Press, 2011), 221.

7. Jean Giroux, "Pro-Life Champions: Phill Kline: a Profile of Rare Courage,"
Celebrate Life Magazine, January–February 2012, https://www.clmagazine
.org/topic/pro-life-champions/phill-kline-a-profile-of-rare-courage/.

Chapter 12: Embrace Their Pain

1. "The 3% Myth: The Abortion Corporation," Live Action, accessed
October 11, 2020, https://www.liveaction.org/learn/3percent/#numbers.

Chapter 14: Find Your Rock

1. Dr. Sheldon Turkish, quoted in "Acuna v. Turkish," Supreme Court of New
Jersey, September 12, 2007, https://casetext.com/case/acuna-v-turkish-6.

2. Monica Burke, "New Report Shows Planned Parenthood Raked in $1.5
Billion in Taxpayer Funds Over 3 Years," The Heritage Foundation, March
12, 2018, https://www.heritage.org/marriage-and-family/commentary
/new-report-shows-planned-parenthood-raked-15-billion-taxpayer-funds.

3. "Undercover Video Exposes Abortion Clinic Misinformation About Fetal
Development," Catholic News Agency, April 13, 2010, https://www
.catholicnewsagency.com/news/undercover_video_exposes_abortion
_clinic_misinformation_about_fetal_development.

4. "Undercover Video Exposes Abortion Clinic Misinformation," Catholic
News Agency.

5. "The Church demands four major characteristics to be exhibited in
the life and works of an early Church leader if he is to be considered a
Father of the Church. These are antiquity, meaning that he lived before
the eighth century (the death of St. John Damascene [cir. A.D. 750]
is generally regarded as the close of the age of the Fathers); doctrinal
orthodoxy; personal sanctity; and approval by the Church." See "Who
Were the Church Fathers?" Catholic Answers, accessed October 12, 2020,
https://www.catholic.com/qa/who-were-the-church-fathers. A church

doctor is a Christian theologian considered authoritative by the Catholic Church.

Chapter 16: Focus

1. Numbers are derived from the Guttmacher Institute and Planned Parenthood: number of total US abortions and number of abortions performed at Planned Parenthood.
2. "Planned Parenthood Rape Cover-Up," Life Institute, accessed October 12, 2020, https://thelifeinstitute.net/learning-centre/abortion-facts /providers/ippf/planned-parenthood-rape-cover-up.
3. "Planned Parenthood Rape Cover-Up," Life Institute.
4. Matthew Balan, "Unlike Big Three Competitors, CNN Covers Planned Parenthood Sting Video," Newsbusters, February 2, 2011, https://www .newsbusters.org/blogs/nb/matthew-balan/2011/02/02/unlike-big -three-competitors-cnn-covers-planned-parenthood-sting.
5. Jon Hurdle and Trip Gabriel, "Philadelphia Abortion Doctor Guilty of Murder in Late-Term Procedures," *New York Times*, May 13, 2013, https:// www.nytimes.com/2013/05/14/us/kermit-gosnell-abortion-doctor-found -guilty-of-murder.html?_r=1&.
6. Erik Eckholm, "Group Releases Hidden Tapes of Planned Parenthood," *New York Times*, February 1, 2011, https://www.nytimes.com/2011/02/02 /us/02parenthood.html.

Chapter 17: Expect Resistance from Within

1. "Public Statement by Eight Alabama Clergymen," April 12, 1963, quoted on Mass Resistance, https://www.massresistance.org/docs/gen/09a/mlk _day/statement.html.
2. Martin Luther King Jr., "Letter from a Birmingham Jail," April 16, 1963, African Studies Center, University of Pennsylvania, https://www.africa .upenn.edu/Articles_Gen/Letter_Birmingham.html.
3. Joe Pistone, *Donnie Brasco: Unfinished Business* (New York: Hachette Book Group, 2008), 50.

Chapter 18: Keep the Pressure On

1. Emma Brockes, "Gloria Steinem: 'If Men Could Get Pregnant, Abortion Would Be a Sacrament," *Guardian*, October 17, 2015, https://www

.theguardian.com/books/2015/oct/17/gloria-steinem-activist-interview
-memoir-my-life-on-the-road.

2. Ginette Paris, *The Sacrament of Abortion* (Thompson, CT: Spring
   Publications, 1998), https://www.amazon.com/Sacrament-Abortion
   -Ginette-Paris/dp/0882143522.

3. "Abortion," Gallup, https://news.gallup.com/poll/1576/abortion.aspx.

Chapter 20: Learn to Pivot

1. Planned Parenthood, *Annual Report 2018–2019*, (New York, 2019), 27,
   https://www.plannedparenthood.org/uploads/filer_public/2e/da/2eda3f50
   -82aa-4ddb-acce-c2854c4ea80b/2018-2019_annual_report.pdf.

2. Dr. Anthony Levatino, "Doctor Walks Away from Performing Abortions
   After Daughter's Death," *Fox & Friends*, February 28, 2019, https://video
   .foxnews.com/v/6008330259001#sp=show-clips.

3. Jeremy W. Peters, "Republicans Alter Script on Abortion, Seeking to Shift
   Debate," *New York Times*, July 26, 2015, https://www.nytimes.com/2015
   /07/27/us/politics/republicans-alter-script-on-abortion-seeking-to-shift
   -debate.html.

4. Dustin Siggins, "Clinton: Planned Parenthood Videos Are 'Disturbing,'"
   LifeSite News, July 29, 2015, https://www.lifesitenews.com/news/clinton
   -planned-parenthood-videos-are-disturbing.

5. "David Daleiden Indicted on Felony Charge by Texas Grand Jury,"
   Planned Parenthood, January 25, 2016, https://www.plannedparenthood
   .org/about-us/newsroom/press-releases/david-daleiden-indicted-on-felony
   -charge-by-texas-grand-jury.

6. Cecile Richards in an interview with ABC News commentator George
   Stephanopoulos, Center for Medical Progress, "Planned Parenthood
   VP Says Fetuses May Come Out Intact, Agrees Payments Specific to the
   Specimen,"11:29, YouTube video, July 30, 2015, https://www.youtube.com
   /watch?v=GWQuZMvcFA8.

Chapter 22: Embrace Mercy

1. Sarah Terzo, "Planned Parenthood Taught Workers to Prevent 'Being
   Recorded' Rather Than Help Abuse Victims," Live Action, June 16, 2018,
   https://www.liveaction.org/news/planned-parenthood-prevent-recorded
   -abuse/.

2. Stephen Vincent, "Bernard Nathanson Dead at 84," *National Catholic Register*, February 21, 2011, https://www.ncregister.com/daily-news /bernard-nathanson-dead-at-84.

3. "Dr. Bernard Nathanson, R.I.P.", Catholic League for Religious and Civil Rights, February 22, 2011, https://www.catholicleague.org/dr-bernard -nathanson-r-i-p/.

4. Live Action, "Former Abortionist Kathi Aultman Speaks Out on Her Pro-Life Conversion," 21:43, YouTube video, June 28, 2019, https://www .youtube.com/watch?v=3-u6v8jp_ys&feature=emb_rel_pause.

Chapter 26: Beware of False Compassion

1. "What is AAPLOG's Position on 'Abortion to Save the Life of the Mother'?," American Association of Pro-Life Obstetricians and Gynecologists, July 2009, https://aaplog.org/what-is-aaplogs-position-on-abortion-to-save-the -life-of-the-mother/.

2. Donna Harrison and Lila Rose, "Abortion Is Never Medically Necessary," *Washington Examiner*, February 26, 2019, https://www.washingtonexaminer .com/opinion/op-eds/abortion-is-never-medically-necessary.

Chapter 27: Begin Anew

1. "Number of Abortions—Abortion Counters," accessed October 13, 2020, http://www.numberofabortions.com.

About the Author

Lila Rose is a speaker, writer, and human rights activist. She founded and serves as president of Live Action, a media and news nonprofit dedicated to ending abortion and inspiring a culture that respects all human life. Lila speaks internationally on family and cultural issues and has addressed members of the European Parliament and the United Nations Commission on the Status of Women. She has been called the face of the millennial pro-life movement and regularly appears on and writes for major news outlets. She also hosts the podcast *The Lila Rose Show*, which addresses topics like purpose, work, relationships, and health.